Rosen, Mark I.
Thank you for being such
a pain

Keep me clean!

Please don't
handle me
with soiled hands.

THANK YOU
FOR BEING
SUCH A PAIN

THANK YOU
FOR BEING
SUCH A PAIN

Spiritual Guidance
for Dealing
with Difficult People

Mark I. Rosen, PH.D.

Harmony Books/NEW YORK

Published by Harmony Books, a division of Crown Publishers, Inc., 201 East 50th Street,
New York, New York 10022. Member of the Crown Publishing Group.

Random House, Inc. New York, Toronto, London, Sydney, Auckland

www.randomhouse.com/

HARMONY and colophon are trademarks of Crown Publishers, Inc.

Printed in the United States of America

Design by Lynne Amft

Library of Congress Cataloging-in-Publication Data
Rosen, Mark I.
Thank you for being such a pain: spiritual guidance for dealing
with difficult people / by Mark I. Rosen.—1st ed.
Includes bibliographical references and index.
1. Interpersonal conflict.   2. Interpersonal relations.
3. Interpersonal conflict—Religious aspects.   4. Interpersonal
relations—Religious aspects.   I. Title.
BF637.I48R67   1998
158.2—dc21   97-23784
                                                        CIP

ISBN 0-609-60099-0

10 9 8 7 6 5 4 3 2

In loving memory of my mother, Etta Rosen, who was always kind, even when others were difficult.

CONTENTS

Contents

INTRODUCTION

I have not written this book to teach the reader anything new. Rather, it is my aim to direct the reader's attention to certain well-known and generally accepted truths, for the very fact that they are well-known and generally accepted is the cause of their being overlooked.

MOSHE HAYYIM LUZZATTO

So begins *The Path of the Upright*, a book written by an Italian rabbi about the spiritual implications of behavior. Though it was first published in Amsterdam in 1740, its opening applies just as readily to the book you are holding.

Thank You for Being Such a Pain is about the difficulties we experience in everyday relationships and the deeper spiritual meanings that underlie them. During our time on earth, very few experiences bring us as much joy or deliver as much sorrow as our relationships with others. From the moment we enter this world, we form relationships, and relationships form us.

Thank You for Being Such a Pain is based on four premises: first, that life's seemingly random encounters are not so random after all; second, that the pain, frustration, and suffering we experience with certain people are just as important for our personal and spiritual growth as love and joy—adversity is our teacher, pushing past our resistance and teaching us what we would fail to otherwise learn; third, that difficult relationships can and should be healed, as learning how to transform enmity is one of our most important life lessons; and fourth, that healing requires being attentive to the spiritual lessons that life presents us—when we do the inner work we are here to do, our outer relationships and circumstances become transformed.

1

Perhaps learning spiritual lessons is not your primary motivation as you begin this book; you have probably picked it up because someone in your life is causing you emotional pain and driving you nuts. Maybe even several someones. They might include your boss, your mother-in-law, your next-door neighbor, or your spouse. You may be suffering quietly or trying very hard to do something about the problem. You may even be seeing a professional therapist or talking with your priest, minister, or rabbi to get some comfort. It hurts, and you want it to stop. You are obsessed, and you'd love to forget about the whole thing, but you can't.

You are looking for a solution. But the real solution does not lie in simply getting the other person to stop annoying you. The best response does not involve retaliation, fighting back, enduring the difficulties, walking away, or giving up. The true resolution comes only when you finally learn what the other person is teaching you.

Your antagonist is indeed a teacher, an unwitting envoy of a universe that wants you to grow. For those who live with a spiritual orientation, life is not a series of haphazard occurrences. The great spiritual traditions all maintain that we live in a magnificent universe, full of meaning. Conflicts that seem to be chance occurrences are actually orchestrated for our spiritual development by an intelligence totally beyond our comprehension. Some call this sacred force God. This may be an unfamiliar notion to you. It may seem preposterous in the face of your anguish or make you uncomfortable, but it is a premise upheld by spiritual teachers and teachings throughout the ages.

In order for you to benefit from this book, it is not necessary that you agree with this premise or possess a spiritual mind-set. Agnostics and atheists will find much to ponder. The suggestions and exercises that follow require no affirmation of belief.

The perspectives that have shaped this book can be traced to two especially difficult relationships that have been lifelong struggles for me. The first, with my father, has happily begun to heal over the past few years. The second, with my own spirituality, continues to baffle, frustrate, and inspire me.

Perhaps the most difficult relationship we can ever have is one we all share, whether or not we accept or realize it. Each of us has a relationship, invariably a difficult one, with the unknowable Supreme Being. Even those who do not believe in an Ultimate Reality cannot ignore this relationship, for deciding to be a nonbeliever involves a conscious choice about the nature of this relationship.

For those who do believe, the relationship comprises all the most troublesome characteristics of a relationship with a difficult person. Conversations are usually one-sided, we rarely get the response we want, and the other party keeps doing unpredictable and inexplicable things to us.

Since the content of this book has been so strongly shaped by my relationship with my father and my spiritual journey, a more complete story will help you to better understand this book's point of view.

On September 8, 1939, the Nazis invaded Stashov, a small town in Poland south of Warsaw. My grandfather, Mordchai Rozencwaig, a grocer who was a pious man and an observant Jew, was eventually expelled, along with the town's entire Jewish population. He perished during a forced march to the Nazi concentration camp known as Treblinka. My father, Samuel, whose friends called him Shmiel, was seventeen at the time of the invasion and an avid athlete. Because of his age and physical condition, he was not sent to an extermination camp. Instead, he and his brother were forced to toil throughout the war for sixteen hours a day in a series of labor camps, building roads, buildings, and munitions for the Nazis. They were finally liberated by Russian soldiers in Therienstadt, a Czechoslovakian extermination camp, on May 10, 1945.

What my father witnessed and experienced was so unspeakable that he was literally unable to talk about it. His pain and horror have never really healed. I didn't learn the full story until the age of forty-three, when he made a videotape describing his experiences for Steven Spielberg's Shoah project.

I knew about his torment from as early as I can remember, not because he shared it with me, but because my mother and others constantly reminded me of what he had been through, most likely as a way to excuse his behavior. While some turn to alcohol or other excesses to obliterate emotional pain, my father found that the fatigue from constant work was his drug. He put in eleven-hour days, seven days a week, without vacations, at the small neighborhood grocery our family owned, a legacy from his father. Then he came home and collapsed in his easy chair. A kind and caring man despite his ordeal, he faithfully attended to his children's basic needs but otherwise was unavailable. Time and emotional support were not his to give.

Growing up, I was often angry with him, but it was an anger tempered by understanding. How does one blame a father for not being present emotionally when one knows so clearly the reasons why? Add to this the constant questions that children of Holocaust survivors invariably ask. Why the Jews? Why six million? How could it have happened? Why wasn't it stopped? Why did my father survive when so many others didn't? Where was God?

Those years with my father taught me, through his past and his presence, to always ask myself why people acted the way they did, and to look with compassion at the suffering that must invariably lie at the root of problem behaviors. I have found this invaluable in my subsequent dealings with other difficult people.

My spiritual explorations have acted as another strong influence on the way I have viewed conflict and relationship difficulties. The spiritual lens through which I view life was an early acquisition. In 1957, at the age of four, after hearing from a

Sunday-school teacher that God was everywhere, I started looking. I have a vivid recollection of myself as a little boy, filled with awe, gazing into the sky at the corner of Lawrence and Broadway in Chicago's Uptown neighborhood where I grew up. Any reader familiar with the area, which is across the street from the Riviera Theater, now a rock-concert hall, is probably chuckling right now at my choice of a site for revelation.

As I grew older, during the 1960s, I found the Judaism I was exposed to as a child inadequate in satisfying my search for God. My bar mitzvah was a typical stand-up performance devoid of any spirituality. I didn't really find any teachings that appealed to me until I started college. There I discovered Eastern philosophy and began to meditate daily. At twenty-one, after graduation, I took on my first full-time job, as a meditation teacher. You can probably imagine my father's inability to see this as suitable employment for a new college graduate and nice Jewish boy.

The Eastern meditation group I was involved with kept me happy and deluded until my late thirties, when all the Jewishness I had suppressed came rushing back during and after a trip to Jerusalem to attend my youngest brother's wedding.

Growing up with a father who had survived the Holocaust had not inspired me to embrace being Jewish; after all, being Jewish had been proven to be hazardous to one's health. Plus, it wasn't fashionable to be Jewish—many of the Jews I knew with strong spiritual leanings had turned East for spiritual sustenance, finding little of interest in a once rich and deeply mystical tradition that had been watered down to appease the demands of a rational twentieth century. It is striking how many current books that draw upon Eastern spiritual teachings have been written by Jews.

The Jewish people have been irrational targets of animosity (and a lot worse) for thousands of years. In my rediscovery of Judaism, I discovered a wonderfully rich body of teachings on difficulties in relationships, both in the Jewish mystical tradition and in the writings of the Hasidic masters. I embraced them eagerly as a way to heal my own painful relationship problems but, just as importantly, as a way to reconnect with my previously abandoned religion.

Relationship difficulties was a theme confined not only to my personal life. On a professional level, I had chosen to pursue a career that involved relationship difficulties in the workplace. I earned both a master's degree and a doctor of philosophy in industrial relations, studying the dynamics of the employment relationship and the conflicts that inevitably arise between employees and management.

Following a distressing and debilitating two-year conflict with my graduate advisor over the final chapter of my doctoral dissertation that almost kept me from completing my Ph.D., I became a college professor in the Boston area. I taught courses on behavior in organizations and on the management of human resources and subsequently launched a management consulting practice.

In 1992, Interface, an adult education center in Cambridge, Massachusetts, asked me to give an evening talk on difficult people at work. I combined my professional training in workplace conflict with my spiritual studies and added my abundant personal experience with difficult people. I studied what other traditions besides Judaism had to say about relationship difficulties, finding consistent themes in Buddhism, Hinduism, and Christianity. Participants loved the workshop. I had unknowingly generated the foundation of this book.

This text is the product of the many workshops I have given since then and draws on the experiences of the many wonderful people who have attended them. They freely shared their stories and gave me helpful feedback in shaping my ideas.

And, of course, the book has also been strongly influenced by my own experiences with the many difficult people who have paraded through my life from my birth onward, leaving me at times desperate for solace and solutions. I share my discoveries and insights with you here.

Fortunately, through a combination of luck and skill, I've managed to heal many difficult relationships over time. I count several people as friends with whom I once had unpleasant adversarial relationships.

Through the process of working through these difficult relationships, I reluctantly learned a great deal about myself, realized some painful truths, and acquired insights into my character flaws and self-centered desires. The process continues; there is always something new to learn. None of this growth would have taken place in the absence of such encounters. I am a wiser and more mature person as a result of my experiences with difficult people, albeit one who has been very much humbled.

I would be less than honest if I didn't also admit to being difficult myself. Certainly not to everyone, and hopefully not all that often, but enough so that I've managed to annoy some and hurt a few. And they've let me know, loudly. What is ironic and yet so indicative of a Universe that wants me to learn and grow is that some of the unpleasant acts I've done to others have later been done to me.

It is my genuine hope that the concepts, stories, exercises, and suggestions in this book will help you in your dealings with difficult people, providing spiritual uplift and comfort. May you be blessed with deep insight and a complete healing.

A Few Remarks About This Book

This book is primarily intended for those struggling with difficult people in their daily lives. While some of the concepts will also be of help to those in an intimate relationship, or to those who have been deeply hurt by someone in the past, this work is not a substitute for individual or couples therapy by a skilled professional. The hurts and complications that some of us face are sometimes just too daunting for us to unravel on our own. Please consider seeking competent help if you need it.

The material that follows is organized into two parts. Part 1, Understanding the Difficulties, contains a variety of perspectives that will give you new insights into your problems with difficult people. It attempts to answer one of the basic questions that we all ask—why is this happening to me? Chapter 1 provides introductory perspectives. In chapter 2, we examine options—what can one do when troubled by an encounter with a difficult person? Chapter 3 presents a set of possible reasons behind difficult behavior as a way to change how these difficulties are viewed. Chapter 4 examines in detail the core idea of this book: that our difficulties are not random but are sent to us for spiritual growth.

Part 2, Healing the Difficulties, presents specific techniques, advice, and recommendations for improving and resolving your difficult relationships. It answers another fundamental question— how can I heal what I'm feeling and make things better? Chapter 5 offers both psychological and spiritual methods for healing the difficulties without the other person being present. Chapter 6 offers suggestions for a face-to-face discussion with a difficult person, and chapter 7 provides guidance for relating to future difficulties from a spiritual vantage point.

Within each chapter are segments of varying length. While the concepts in this book unfold in linear fashion, it is also possible to read only the sections that are of interest to you, since they are self-contained.

Each chapter ends with a section called Explorations, comprising exercises that will help you delve more deeply into the concepts you've read about. If you plan to do the exercises, you may want to acquire a separate notebook for privacy and so that you have enough space in which to write.

For many years, I noticed how every nonfiction book I read that contained stories of a personal nature began with a statement about how names had been changed to protect the individual's privacy. Having collected such stories, I now understand why, so I've also been careful to change names and details. Some of the stories are composites of several different people's narratives in order to better illustrate a particular point. I also include some of my own stories about difficult people, inspired by the Dalai Lama, whose autobiography *Freedom in Exile* describes in factual terms what the Chinese did to Tibet and the Tibetan people.

I've had great fun locating relevant quotations to begin each section. I regret that some of them are politically incorrect with respect to gender. Once, at a workshop, after I had apologized for the male pronouns in some of the quotations, a woman sternly suggested to me that it was about time I replaced them!

I didn't. What I did was to find as many relevant quotes from women as I could. I hope you are able to overlook the sexist language of writers such as William Shakespeare or Mark Twain and appreciate their pithy insights. There are no replacements for genius.

In the Notes section at the end of this book, I've indicated, whenever practical, where a particular idea originated. I've also provided suggestions for further reading.

While this is a book about relationships, it is also a book about spirituality. I find it very difficult to write about spiritual ideas without reference to a concept of God. For me, trying to write a book with a spiritual message that avoids references to a Supreme Reality is like trying to write a cookbook without references to food.

Still, I have made an effort to be sensitive to the varied notions of God that we all carry. In the course of my studies and teaching, I have met many people who carry a negative concept of God because of the way religion was taught to them in their early years. Pediatric religion, in my opinion, is the single biggest reason why New Age concepts of spirituality have for many supplanted traditional religious practices. Issues regarding God's gender, which my dear friend Rabbi David Zeller likes to call "God below the belt," also evoke many strong reactions.

In an attempt to avoid these negative reactions, I alternate the terms Universe and Holy One in this book with the term God. Holy One (in Hebrew, *HaKadosh Baruch Hu*) is my personal favorite among the many names of God in the liturgy of my own tradition, simultaneously conveying divinity and unity. Feel free to substitute your own terminology if you so desire.

As a final introductory comment, I feel the compulsion to answer an uncomfortable question I've been asked more than once: "Do you actually practice what you recommend?" I would love to say that I did. The reality is that I try and regularly fall short. What you are about to read represents the ideals I strive toward, based on the teachings of the great religious traditions. I take consolation in the thought that if we all at least tried, even if we regularly fell short, the world would be a little less difficult and a little more loving.

PART I

UNDERSTANDING THE DIFFICULTIES

CHAPTER 1

FRIENDS AND FAMILY, ENEMIES AND STRANGERS

Difficult People: There's No Escaping Them

The Bible tells us to love our neighbors, and also to love our enemies; probably because they are generally the same people.

G. K. CHESTERTON

A coworker who persists in telling you every small detail of her lackluster life. A neighbor who responds to your third complaint about barking dogs by hanging up the phone. Cousins who boast about their new vacation home even after learning you've just been laid off and might have to face foreclosure.

Difficult people bedevil us. They sap our energy and distract us, causing us minor annoyance and major distress. We protest, complain, and struggle to cope—sometimes successfully, often uselessly. Many a psychotherapist has built a practice offering advice about how to deal with difficult people, because each of us grapples with at least one such boss, neighbor, or relative.

While the circumstances of interpersonal difficulties may differ, the theme is ever the same. People have been making other people miserable for thousands of years. The Bible is filled with stories of people who do terrible things to each other. Every time we deal with a difficult person, we face one of the dilemmas of being human.

When you are struggling with a difficult person, know that you are not alone. Many before you have faced similar struggles, and many share them with you now. Know also that you will face difficult people in the future. There's no escaping them.

What Makes Someone Difficult?

Ninety-nine percent of the people in the world are fools and the rest of us are in great danger of contagion.

THORNTON WILDER

One of the fascinations of writing this book has been listening to the stories I've been told. People have shared the most outrageous, hilarious, and heartbreaking tales about what difficult people have done to them.

Marlene, who cleans houses, told me about the time her husband gave her entire wardrobe to Goodwill after she announced she was filing for divorce. Gerald, a journalist, spoke about a newspaper editor who was so despised by his staff that when he died they all came to the funeral just to make sure he was really dead. And John, an attorney, described how his new law partner took advantage of him by contriving an elaborate financial scam while he was on vacation. The resulting mess practically bankrupted him and left him legally entangled for years.

One newspaper story I ran across described a contest for the worst boss. The winner was a man who sent his secretary to the bar up the street at the close of work each day to scout for women he could hit on.

The people who do these things to us come in many different forms. Bullies use their power to intimidate. Back-stabbers are pleasant in person but do terrible things in our absence. Know-it-alls are always right. Hotheads explode at the slightest provocation. The list of difficult types is almost endless, as are the many words, both colorful and unprintable, used to describe them.

A difficult person can be a stranger, a neighbor, a teacher, a member of the clergy, someone at work, a relative, or a spouse. One can have a brief but unpleasant encounter or live through a lifetime of woe.

Difficult people make us feel miserable. They refuse to give us our due, or they ridicule, ignore, or disappoint us, hurt our pride, take things from us, lie and deceive, mistreat and betray.

We love to talk about these people. We do it at the coffee shop, we do it in therapy, we do it on radio talk shows. Some of us call them names, others look for a sympathetic ear, and almost everyone wants advice.

We suffer mightily from them. We get depressed, we get angry, we give up. Some of us just stew in silence, others plot revenge, and once in a while we just scream in frustration.

But, no matter how different each circumstance may seem, all of them have one thing in common: Each time we have an encounter with a difficult person, we have an uncomfortable emotional reaction.

The definition of a difficult person is deceptively simple. A difficult person is anyone whose words or actions evoke unwanted and unpleasant emotions.

So, no matter who it is, and no matter what is being done to us, a difficult person is someone who causes us to feel things we'd rather not be feeling.

Why Do Some People Drive Us Crazy?

The art of being wise is the art of knowing what to overlook.

WILLIAM JAMES

Who we find difficult and who doesn't bother us is different for each person. Suppose Sam dislikes people who talk during the movies. They bother him so much that he thinks they should be tied up with licorice whips and bombarded with stale popcorn and half-empty soft-drink cups. He'd like to see all movie blabbers taken into a dark room and "shushed" by a horde of uniformed ushers with bright flashlights until they take an oath never to talk during the movies again.

But people who talk during movies don't bother Sallie one bit. When Sallie was in college, she would go to the movies on campus just to shout at the screen along with all the other students who were there for the same reason. She loves to listen to other people's jaded comments. Movies just aren't any fun unless someone behind her is making colorful remarks about the characters, the dialogue, or the plot.

In both cases, the others' behaviors are identical, but Sam's reaction and Sallie's are at opposite ends of the spectrum. Could it be that difficult people exist in the eye (or ear) of the beholder?

Given this perspective, we can begin to understand why a person isn't difficult just because of what he does. People are difficult, as our previous definition suggests, when we experience unpleasant emotions as a result of their behavior.

It is natural to focus on the apparent cause of our distress. But this is a distraction. Our real focus should be on ourselves. We need to look at our own feelings and our own responses to difficult people's behaviors. We need to ask ourselves why we are reacting so strongly.

An important starting point for dealing with difficult people is to pay attention to what is going on inside us, not just to what the difficult person is doing.

Ways of Seeing

The world is as you are.

MAHARISHI MAHESH YOGI

We like to think that we see the world clearly. We are invested in believing that our view of reality is accurate. So when someone does something that we consider difficult, our interpretation of the situation becomes our truth.

If only it were that simple. In actuality, there are several truths. There is our truth, the truth of the person with whom we're having the difficulties, and the truth of any witnesses or bystanders. Each has a different take on the situation, and each is convinced that his or her interpretation is the most accurate. The Japanese movie classic *Rashomon,* directed by Akira Kurosawa in 1950, explores this theme by showing a crime over and over again, each time from the perspective of one of the involved parties. And each story is radically different.

When we view our difficulties, our interpretations are based on how we feel at the moment. If we are tired, or angry, or suspicious, we will experience an interaction with a difficult person differently than when we're feeling good. Our view of our difficulties is also based on our history. All of our life experience, all of our hurts and mistakes and previous encounters, affect the way we see things now.

When dealing with a difficult person, it is important that you be open to new ways of viewing the situation. If your current perceptions and assumptions about the difficulties were entirely

accurate, you would probably have been able to solve your problem by now.

Why Do Relationships Have Difficulties?

The sword does not feel the wound.

PHILLIP PAUL HALLIE

A friend of mine once made an offhand comment that relationships were so complex she wondered how anyone managed to make them work. Indeed, those of us in the throes of painful relationship difficulties often despair at solutions. But we apparently haven't given up all hope, or we wouldn't pick up books like this one.

While there are many reasons that difficulties arise in our relationships, three are fundamental: insensitivity, inadequate communication, and lack of caring. If Barney doesn't think about others, if he doesn't know how others feel about what he does, and if he doesn't care once he finds out, Barney is a good candidate for being difficult.

Words and actions are powerful; every time we say or do something to someone else we have an effect on that person. Ideally the effect is positive, creating a loving and uplifting feeling. On occasion, it is destructive and can be deeply hurtful. Most of the time, it's somewhere in between.

Sensitivity is the capacity to anticipate and appreciate another's feelings. If we are sensitive, we have a good "sense" of how our words and actions affect someone else. Sensitivity serves as an inner guide to action and speech. If we are insensitive, difficulties arise in our relationships, since we act and speak in ways that do not consider the other person's reactions.

But being sensitive is not enough to prevent difficulties in relationships. Sensitivity has limits; it is always unconfirmed and never infallible. Jim might care about Joan, have the best intentions for her, and think he is anticipating her feelings and needs but still not be helpful. Joan is the only person who is in a position to decide whether Jim has in fact been helpful or hurtful.

Communication is vital; we must listen to and even ask for feedback from others so that we know how they actually feel about what we say and do. If we hurt someone inadvertently, and they don't say ouch, we might do it again out of ignorance. If someone lets us know that they appreciate something we've done, then we know we've done the right thing and will do it again.

Of course, if someone says ouch and we ignore what we hear because we really don't care, difficulties in the relationship can only escalate.

Because some of us can be insensitive, we sometimes do things without giving thought to their repercussions. Because many of us don't speak up about how we feel or don't ask how others feel, people continue to drive us crazy or we continue to drive them crazy. And because there are times when we just don't care, difficulties persist; no one wants to be treated with indifference.

Overcoming our difficulties in relationships requires that we work on developing sensitivity, communication, and caring.

Everyone Is Difficult to Someone

I am firm. You are obstinate. He is a pig-headed fool.

KATHERINE WHITEHORN

Everyone is difficult to someone. Even you. If you are honest with yourself, you have to admit that at one time or another you've done something to drive someone crazy.

Most of us, most of the time, have absolutely no idea that we are doing so. But some of us are experts at it, and a few even take pleasure in it.

Yet no matter how annoying we are to others, we do not willingly accept being labeled as difficult. When we do something to annoy someone else, we're not being difficult; we see it as justified.

"I had a bad day," we assert. "I didn't mean it," we plead. "I didn't do anything," we maintain. "You deserved it," we insist. "You made me do it," we rationalize.

What's really going on is a desire to preserve our self-image. It's a lot easier to focus on another person's behavior than it is to admit that we're being difficult.

Admitting the effects of our own behaviors on others would mean identifying with the very behaviors we condemn. It would mean that we could no longer pretend that we were better than the person who was causing our pain. It would mean that difficult people weren't that different from us; in fact, they *are* us.

To understand our encounters with difficult people, we eventually need to accept the fact that we are them.

A Spiritual Perspective

There is a plan to the universe. There is a high intelligence, maybe even a purpose, but it's given to us on the installment plan.
ISAAC BASHEVIS SINGER

I began playing tennis several times a weeks after high school when I found a regular partner, the son of the local Methodist minister. Ted and I would walk to the public courts at Winnemac Park in Chicago, whack some balls around on the cracked asphalt surface, and head back to the parsonage where he lived. We'd listen to the latest rock music while his sisters practiced piano and sang very proper Christian music in rehearsal for the upcoming Sunday church service. I was treated warmly, almost as a Jewish curiosity.

As a tennis player, my forehand was adequate, my serve passable, and my backhand rickety. I enjoyed playing with Ted, but my strokes didn't improve until a few years later, when I began to play against people who took the game more seriously. One opponent spotted my lame backhand and began to target all his shots to my left side. I was forced to improve my backhand. Another won because I was out of shape. He wore me out by making me run all over, skillfully scattering his returns around the court until my trotting eventually slowed to a fatigued totter. I worked on building my endurance, cursing his talent between increasingly labored breaths each time we played.

I liked playing with Ted because we were good friends, we had fun, and because it wasn't very demanding. I was less fond of playing with my other partners, who turned something I enjoyed into hard work. I needed to remind myself that my game was improving under their pressure.

The same sort of pattern emerged in graduate school. I tended to like the classes taught by professors who were entertaining and not too demanding. Other classes, the ones with challenging topics and relentless workloads, were agonizing. One class in particular was notorious, taught by a professor who had no interest in real-world issues and a sadistic bent toward impossibly complex statistics. I was amused to read a reminiscence of his class in a recent alumni newsletter that compared the camaraderie among the students to the community spirit that tends to emerge during a natural disaster.

Yet looking back, I realize that I learned far more from the hard classes, and the learning stayed with me. For both tennis and school, there wasn't much of an association between how things felt inside and what I ultimately learned.

I find it useful to think of the difficult people in my life as being like skilled tennis opponents or tough professors. I don't like what they do, I don't like how I feel, but I recognize that they provide me with an unmatched opportunity to improve myself, one that is available nowhere else.

The mistake I used to make, and the mistake that many of us continue to make, is to judge life by our subjective experience. If it feels good, if it makes us happy, if it doesn't yank us out of our comfort zone, it's good, and we pursue it. If it scares us, pushes us to the limit, angers us, or threatens our complacency, it's bad, and we avoid it. Having such a mind-set can mislead us. Our minds may have a natural tendency to seek pleasant experiences, but that doesn't mean we're headed in a positive direction.

Having intense emotional reactions to difficult people is both normal and desirable—in fact, I would start to wonder about those who didn't react this way. But having a negative emotional reaction doesn't necessarily mean that something bad is happening to you. The two do not always go hand in hand.

Suppose you were able to escape your emotional dungeon and observe your difficult relationships with complete objectivity. You might realize that your nemesis was actually helping you to develop qualities that had been dormant, or getting you in touch with some previously frozen feelings, or enabling you to understand yourself in ways that were previously inaccessible. If you'll permit me to stretch my tennis metaphor, difficult people help you to improve your interpersonal backhand, develop your emotional forehand, and strengthen your spiritual serve.

You have every right to grit your teeth, swear, yell, complain, and act as if you don't believe any of this while you're in the midst of a painful encounter with a difficult person. It took me a long time and lots of anguish before I came around to seeing my plight in this new and ultimately uplifting way. However, I confess to drawing heavily on my spiritual beliefs, and I can certainly appreciate that you may not share these beliefs.

But for the sake of further inquiry, let's consider as a working assumption the possibility that truly difficult people don't just randomly show up in our lives. Let's suppose they are *sent* to us.

Difficult people, according to this viewpoint, are teachers who help us to develop in a fashion that can only take place when we are forced to face and surmount an unwelcome challenge. Difficult people impel us to rise to the occasion.

We are not on this earth just to have fun, although that is one of the bonuses of being human. We are here to develop our talents, refine our character, and contribute our utterly unique and divine essence toward the greater good. No one else can do what we are here to do.

The catch is that we can't make our contribution to this cosmic scheme if we're not ready. There are things we must learn; it is likely that we can't learn at least some of them without a divine kick in the spiritual butt.

So, I ask you to give serious consideration to the possibility that the Universe delivers unto us the ideal foe, a person whose characteristics exactly correspond to the places within us that need learning and healing.

The suffering we endure may not make any sense to us at the time, but in retrospect, if we search within ourselves for meaning, we will eventually come to the realization that we have been transformed by the encounter in a necessary way.

It is not possible to prove this to you; I ask that you consider this way of viewing your relationships with an open mind and a receptive heart. As you learn more about this perspective in the course of reading this book, assess its value for yourself in your dealings with difficult people.

The great spiritual traditions all teach that we live in a meaningful, purposeful, and loving universe. Later in this book I'll attempt to describe what these teachings have to say about the indispensable role of difficult relationships in our spiritual development.

It is helpful to consider the possibility that difficult people are sent to us to help our spiritual growth. Our task is not to focus on the person causing the problem, but to look within ourselves and understand why we are having these problems and what we are supposed to be learning on our spiritual journey. Difficult people help to reveal the spaces inside us that need remodeling.

Explorations

TAKING INVENTORY

Purpose: To help you identify patterns or trends in your difficult relationships

The following exercise will serve as a foundation for many of the concepts presented in this book. You'll want to spend at least half an hour working on it—or more, depending on how many difficult people you have in your life.

I've called the exercise Taking Inventory, because it is designed to give you an overview of the difficult people currently in your life. The idea is to identify patterns and trends.

You'll find it helpful to use the chart on page 27 as a model. I suggest that you make your own, larger version instead of writing in this book. Some of what you'll be writing you probably won't want anyone else to see. Here are instructions for each column heading:

Name and Age	Write the person's name or initials and approximate age.
Male or Female	List the difficult person's gender.
Work or Home	Do you encounter this difficult person at work or in your personal life?
How Often?	How often does the person affect you? All the time, periodically, or occasionally?
When?	When are you affected by this difficult person? For example, does it happen randomly? After drinking? Only when you are tired? Hungry? When you are under stress? When the person ignores you? Criticizes you? When you have to work together and coordinate efforts?
Your Feelings	What is your emotional response to this person's behavior? For example, are you angry? Do you feel bad about yourself? Do you feel taken advantage of? Do you think about revenge?
Negative Traits	What is it about the person that bothers you so much? For example, is the person conceited? Stubborn? Critical and judgmental? Selfish?

When you're done completing the chart, look for patterns. You might find the following questions helpful:

- Are the difficult people in your life mainly men or women?
- Are the difficult people in your life primarily older, the same age, or younger than you?
- Do you encounter the difficult people in your life primarily at work or at home?
- Do work difficulties spill over into your personal life?
- Do difficult people in your personal life affect your work?
- Are you under stress from several difficult people at the same time?

- Do the same feelings tend to come up consistently in you in response to several different people?
- Are you bothered by the same negative traits in several difficult people?
- Do any of the patterns remind you of people in your past?

When you're done, if patterns are present, you should be able to spot them. For example, you might find that you tend to have problems with older women at work who are critical, and you feel inadequate as a result. Or you might find that you only have difficulties with a particular person after a couple of drinks. These are clues that will help you to better understand your difficulties. Any patterns that you identify will start to give you information about your personal areas of vulnerability and the places that you need to heal.

TAKING INVENTORY

Name and Age	Male or Female	Work or Home	How Often?	When?	Your Feelings	Negative Traits

CHAPTER 2

OPTIONS FOR DEALING WITH DIFFICULT PEOPLE

Choices

We are spinning our own fates, good or evil, and never to be undone. Every smallest stroke of virtue or of vice leaves its never so little scar. . . .

WILLIAM JAMES

Okay, enough philosophy. You're reading this book because you want advice. You want to *do something*. You want me to tell you how to make it go away. You're exasperated. You're obsessed. You wish it was over so you could get back to living your life.

I hear you. So let's consider six possible things you could do—six potential courses of action.

First, maybe you could just ignore the whole thing. Pretend it isn't there, avoid dealing with it, and act as if everything is fine. You wouldn't be the first—lots of people do nothing all the time. In other words, maybe the best thing to do might be not to do anything.

Second, you could make nice. Put harmony above everything else and find a way, somehow, to go along with other people's

unacceptable behaviors. Work actively to keep them happy by giving them what they want. Be a pleaser.

Third, you could do whatever was necessary to get the
offending person out of your life. Walk away. Leave. Go somewhere else. Quit. Get a divorce. Tell the person to get lost and
never darken your door again.

Fourth, what about getting even? That's why we have a legal
system. Or take things into your own hands and give them a dose
of their own medicine. That would teach them. You'd show them a
thing or two. Just thinking about revenge brings to mind all sorts
of delicious and diabolical ideas. Your imagination is already working overtime. I'm assuming we both agree that foul play, a favorite
choice of mystery writers and front-page stories, is not an acceptable inclusion in this category and not an option under any circumstances.

Fifth, how about talking things over? Maybe it's possible to get
the person to stop. Or start. Or change. You could negotiate some
kind of solution to the conflict. If the person acted differently,
changed what he or she was doing, considered your feelings, it
wouldn't be so bad. That's another possibility to consider.

And sixth, what if you could make some inner changes? What
if you could look at the situation in a new way that would give you
fresh insights and perspectives? What if you could use it as an
opportunity to learn more about yourself and become a better
person? What if you could give spiritual meaning to your struggles? What if you could just rise above the problem?

Let's spend some time exploring the implications of each
course of action. They are certainly not equal in their effects.

When dealing with a difficult person, you can do things that
leave the situation unchanged, you can do things that make it
worse, or you can do things that make it better. Give careful
thought to the course of action you choose. The results of your

actions may not be totally predictable, but they are definitely not random and can have long-lasting repercussions.

You can't choose the thoughts and feelings that come to you about a difficult person. You do, however, have a choice in how you respond.

Doing Nothing

The House of Peers, throughout the war,
Did nothing in particular,
And did it very well.

GILBERT AND SULLIVAN (*Iolanthe,* Act II)

Our first option in dealing with a difficult person is to ignore the difficulties, avoid discussing them, pretend they aren't happening and stifle whatever feelings arise within us.

Lots of people do this every day. It's the only way they manage to survive. Some people do it so well that avoidance and denial become their primary method of dealing with problems in relationships. I once knew a woman who didn't speak to her husband for six months after a fight. She lived in the same house with him the whole time.

Avoidance is appropriate for one particular type of situation. If one has no hope of ever improving a difficult relationship, then dealing with it by not dealing with it is perfectly logical. If there is no chance that it will get better, there is no point in trying to make it better.

Unfortunately, the feeling of hopelessness that leads to avoidance is often a residue of the past and not an indicator of the present. If, growing up, one's needs were unmet and concerns ignored, one is likely to assume that the world will respond the same way now as it did before. Hence the tendency to avoid dealing with problems in relationships, since one automatically assumes such efforts will be futile.

The trick is to let go of the past and deal with each new circumstance in the moment. Of course, this is easier said than done.

There are two basic reasons why avoidance as a way of dealing with difficult people doesn't work. The first is that people problems usually don't get better by themselves; by doing nothing, we tend to perpetuate the problem. And second, we pay a price for not expressing our feelings. They don't go away, they just keep churning around inside us.

Sometimes these unexpressed feelings surface in our behaviors. We might eat too much, gamble to excess, buy things we don't need and/or can't afford, drink or take drugs because we're not dealing with the negative feelings we have about the people who cause us grief.

Sometimes these unexpressed feelings manifest themselves in our bodies. In the workshops I give that form the basis of this book, I lead an eyes-closed exercise. During this exercise, and often for the first time, people experience bodily sensations—tension in their shoulders, soreness in their neck muscles, or tightness in their chest—associated with their relationship problems. In actuality, these somatic responses are always present, but until the exercise sparks the connection, people often fail to associate them with unresolved feelings about a difficult relationship.

We can take this concept a scary step further. Medicine has learned enough about the connections between mind and body to statistically link unexpressed emotions with a variety of illnesses. Cancer, heart disease, and other silent slayers have been found to be correlated with negative emotional states.

There is one situation in which doing nothing makes sense, and that is when two parties need a cooling-off period. When emotions are intense, it is sometimes wise to wait before acting. But in these circumstances, we do not avoid or deny the difficulties; we instead make a conscious choice and in actuality do something by doing nothing.

So, while every so often it may be a good idea to do nothing if the situation calls for it, most of the time this is not a very healthy option for dealing with difficult people.

By avoiding your problems with other people, you only create more problems for yourself.

Making Nice

Patience, n. A minor form of despair, disguised as a virtue.
A M B R O S E B I E R C E

All of us have found ourselves in situations where the easiest thing to do is to grin and bear it. No matter how inappropriate the other person's behavior might be, if we just smile, endure, and let the other person have his way, we'll get through it somehow. Rather than pretending there isn't a problem, we make a choice to deal with it by making nice.

In my management-consulting practice, I regularly hear stories about bosses and customers from hell. What the employees relating these stories are able to endure always amazes me.

One client, the manager of a four-star restaurant at a majestic Cape Cod seaside resort, related a story about an elderly guest one summer who invariably sent back his gourmet selection, complaining it was inedible. Not content to simply complain about the food, he also took pains to insult the person serving it. Three different servers were consecutively reduced to tears and refused to serve him again. Finally the manager decided to serve him herself the next time he came in.

She was polite and solicitous as only the manager of an expensive restaurant can be. This seemed to make him even nastier.

After receiving several minutes of especially courteous treatment, he snarled, "Wipe that disgusting smile off your face—I don't want to see your teeth anymore." She cried, too.

Appeasement can sometimes be effective in the short term, especially when the preservation of a relationship is paramount. This customer was wrong, but we all know that in the world of business, customers are always right. Keeping customers happy so that they keep coming back is more important than winning a point. In our personal relationships as well, it sometimes makes sense to let other people get their way to maintain harmony and avoid conflict, especially when the issues are trivial to us but significant to them. Many things just aren't important enough to make a fuss about.

It may also be wise to say yes to someone now in order to get a yes back from them in the future, as long as both parties agree to the arrangement. For example, you might decide to go along when your spouse wants to see a movie that you know is awful because you want to go to a play together next weekend. If you take this approach, be careful—it is likely to backfire if the arrangement is not explicitly discussed.

Sometimes we are forced to give in if the other person holds all the cards. When someone has power over us, going along with his or her demands may be our only choice.

However, in the long term, we pay a huge price for always acceding to the demands of others. People take advantage of us, and our anger builds. Once difficult people realize we always end up saying yes, they will expect and demand more and more. And the more our needs are not met, the more resentful we will feel. You always end up losing out when you continue to be nice to someone who isn't.

If you have a tendency to be a nice-maker, who gives in to others to avoid conflict, give careful consideration to the price you are paying.

So, when is it advisable to make nice? For a one-time encounter, or when an issue is trivial, or when it is important to maintain harmony, or when we want to earn credits for the future, or when we lack power, giving in may be an appropriate response. But if a relationship is to survive and thrive over time, and if we don't want to be a doormat, giving in is not a good idea.

It doesn't always make sense to make nice.

Leaving

Hello, I must be going.
I cannot stay, I came to say, I must be going.
I'm glad I came, but just the same,
I must be going.

SUNG BY GROUCHO MARX
IN THE MOVIE *Animal Crackers*

Leaving can solve a lot of relationship problems. You have a boss who screams at you so often you wouldn't recognize his voice at a normal volume? Quit. You have a boyfriend who's so cheap that his idea of a birthday dinner is taking you to McDonald's? Dump him. Your neighbor's house is the local headquarters for a biker gang? Move.

Not so fast, unless you're planning a Groucho imitation.

Have you ever acted abruptly and made a spontaneous decision to leave? Anyone who has ever dramatically said, "I quit," at work or, "This is good-bye," in a relationship knows what I'm talking about. Generally, when we leave under these circumstances, we leave lots of unfinished business and plenty of pieces to pick up later.

When the going gets tough, the temptation to get going looms large. We have a natural inclination to avoid continuing discomfort by distancing ourselves from its source. The problem is that sometimes discomfort is good for us.

Yes, you heard me right. There are times when sticking it out is the very best thing one can do. So the key question is, when does it make sense to leave, and when does it make sense to stay?

That depends on whether you tend to be a leaver or a stayer. Each of us has our own way of dealing with separation and loss, and our individual style may be a more important consideration than the situation we find ourselves in.

Some people are tempted to leave at the first sign of trouble no matter what the situation. Their inclination is to move on when things get rocky.

Marilyn, a woman I once worked with, wanted badly to get married, but her relationships never lasted longer than a few months. As soon as any problem developed with a new boyfriend, her fatal-flaw detector went on alert, and she inevitably found several reasons not to pursue the relationship. Soon thereafter, the boyfriend was history.

What Marilyn hadn't yet learned is that shared interests like old movies or dancing aren't sufficient to sustain a successful intimate relationship. Intimacy requires the ability to acknowledge, discuss, and resolve the various problems that every relationship encounters. Conflict of any kind made Marilyn uncomfortable. She didn't know how to deal with it, so she avoided it altogether by finding a seemingly valid excuse for leaving every time it appeared.

Leavers like Marilyn run away not from the situation but from their own feelings. Any situation that triggers inner discomfort is interpreted as an external threat to be avoided rather than a personal issue to be resolved.

Leavers also tend to leave because they are overly optimistic. Leavers think the grass is greener somewhere else; leavers are the ones who chase the pot of gold at the end of the rainbow.

So, if you are a leaver, it might be wiser for you *not* to leave when relationship problems arise. The situation may present a golden opportunity for you to face your fears and heal your emotions. It could also provide you with a chance to learn to appreciate what you have rather than always being on the lookout for something better.

Being a stayer can be just as problematic. Stayers are people who stick around long after the parade has passed. Stayers are people who hold on far longer than they should.

Stayers need to learn to take better care of themselves by leaving untenable situations. So if, looking back at your own history, you find that you tend to stick it out much too long, you might want to work on recognizing problem situations early so that you can leave before things reach the point of harm.

Anxiety over the unknown is one reason why stayers stay. While their current situation might range from bad to abominable, stayers are even more afraid of what things might be like if they left. Stayers think it better to endure an uncomfortable but familiar present than to take a chance on an unfamiliar future.

Some people stay because of a longstanding commitment to a person or situation. Loyalty can be a strong interpersonal glue. Other people stay in difficult relationships for economic reasons, or because they have low self-esteem and unconsciously feel that they deserve to be mistreated.

What if you're not someone who runs away prematurely or sticks around for too long? What if you're somewhere in the middle? On what basis do you decide that you've had enough?

All of us have agonized over this question. We've considered whether to leave or stay regarding places to live, jobs, even marriages. Easy answers elude us.

But there are several different ways of looking at a given situation that may prove helpful.

The first question to ask concerns unfinished business. If you were to leave, how much would remain unresolved between you and the other person? Is leaving the best and only way to resolve these difficulties? If you were to leave, would the person and the problems continue to live inside your head?

Leaving isn't necessarily the best solution for resolving unfinished business. If you leave a difficult situation with another person without a sincere attempt to resolve the difficulties first, the specific problem may come to an end, but the deeper issues that created the problem in the first place won't be resolved.

Ricardo, a software engineer, had a job he loved, except for the relationship he had with his boss. Ricardo worked largely on his own, developing state-of-the-art software products, and his sophisticated skills were legendary at the firm where he worked. Yet even though Ricardo's knowledge was far superior to that of Curt, his boss, Curt insisted on closely supervising each project. Curt questioned Ricardo extensively, challenged his assumptions, and asked him to justify the time he spent on each phase. Curt wanted him to constantly demonstrate that what he was working on would be attractive to consumers and profitable to the firm.

Ricardo hated the way Curt looked over his shoulder. Finally he had had enough of what he viewed as Curt's nonstop interference and lack of respect for his expertise. So he left the firm for a smaller company, where he was given complete autonomy to develop new products. Six months later, the owner of this company sold out to a much larger firm.

Ironically, Ricardo soon found himself in exactly the same situation as before. The new corporate managers were even more insistent that he justify his efforts, since they were combing the new acquisition for ways to cut costs.

Ricardo had failed to learn a basic lesson about work—one cannot do whatever one wants, no matter how brilliantly, when someone else signs the paycheck. Curt wasn't a busybody—he was just doing his job. He himself was responsible to higher-ups for all the employees he managed and needed to justify his budgetary expenditures.

Have you ever noticed how the same type of problem tends to arise for you in a variety of situations? When you're thinking of leaving a situation involving personal conflict, ask yourself if the issues are similar to those you have encountered elsewhere. If so, consider it likely that you will continue to encounter these issues until you finally understand and work through them. If you stick around and deal with them in the present, they are less likely to pose unpleasant problems for you in the future.

A second question to ask about whether to leave or stay is more straightforward. Do the benefits of leaving outweigh the costs?

Sometimes the pain we are experiencing in a particular situation impels us to leave, but we haven't carefully considered the alternatives. Leaving makes sense if we know we are leaving for something better, but not if we are leaving just for the sake of getting away. When an unknown future lies ahead of us, we need to know our options and formulate a plan of action.

Ultimately, the question of whether to stay or leave should not be governed solely by our anticipated pain or pleasure, emotions usually at the heart of any decision. Consider also whether you will learn more by staying or leaving. Which choice gives you more of an opportunity to learn about yourself and how you function in relationships? Which choice will best help you to grow as a person and overcome your limitations? Can you endure the discomfort in order to extract the wisdom that is hidden in every life challenge?

> **The decision to tough it out or take a hike is one of our most difficult choices. There is no wrong choice, because we learn from both. Either choice may help us to become a better person or offer us experiences that will help the next time we find ourselves in a similar situation.**

Getting Even and Fighting Back

I'll get you, my pretty, and your little dog, too!

THE WICKED WITCH TO DOROTHY

IN *The Wizard of Oz*

As a new freshman at the University of Illinois, I was assigned to a dormitory inhabited by a collection of crude, rowdy, and drunken students. While they regularly harassed residents in assorted ways, on one particularly inebriated evening they really decided to have some fun—at my expense. Around midnight, I awoke to find seven of them encircling my bed; I had gone to sleep early so that I would be fresh for a final exam early the next morning. They grabbed me and carried me, pajama clad, struggling and swearing, into the communal bathroom, and threw me in the shower, making sure the water was ice-cold. I ended up shivering and enraged. They thought it was a great prank.

I never quite got up enough courage to get even, but I sure wanted to, and my eighteen-year-old mind was obsessed with thoughts of revenge. My favorite fantasy had superglue as its central ingredient. It was to be strategically applied to the doorjambs of the rooms of my assailants in the middle of the night, once each occupant had gone to bed after an evening of serious beer drinking. To appreciate the full depravity of this contemplated act of vengeance, it might help if I remind you that there were no private bathrooms.

Regina Barreca, in her book *Sweet Revenge,* provides a variety of wickedly entertaining revenge stories. My favorite, surprising for its perpetrator, involves a priest who always put garlic in the food he cooked because he knew how much his bishop disliked it. The bishop had made him miserable, and he felt he had to do something, however trivial, to get even.

The desire for revenge would appear to be both universal

and ancient. When wronged by someone, it is a rare person who doesn't at least consider evening the score. And of course there are those who act on their thoughts. Regrettably, some of their stories make the evening news.

There are three basic motives for taking revenge: to make ourselves feel better, to send a message, and to avert further harm.

Revenge is often seen as a primary way to purge unwanted and unpleasant emotions. If, for example, someone has lied to, betrayed, or humiliated us, we are stuck with feelings we want badly to get rid of. Revenge would seem to offer a way to transform these intolerable feelings. For the most part, revenge does make one feel better. There is for many an unfortunate joy in seeing others receive their comeuppance. The German language even has a special word, *schadenfreude*, for taking joy in others' pain.

The problem with using revenge to feel better is that the good feelings are only temporary and illusory. Over time, if we have any kind of a conscience, we tend to feel worse. It's hard to continue feeling good about being bad.

The second motive for seeking revenge is to send a message to the other party. Depending on the sender's level of rage, the message is usually something like, "Ouch, that hurt, you ———, and here's what it felt like!" In this mode, revenge is most effective when the difficult person gets a dose of her own medicine. Our secret hope is that others will see the error of their ways once they realize what it feels like and come to us with genuine remorse for what they've done.

We all know this rarely happens. At best, the difficult person may realize how miserable she's made us as she reflects upon her own distress at our hands. The problem is, she usually doesn't care about our misery. If she did, she wouldn't have done the thing in the first place that made us want to dangle her out a window.

Revenge must be done with finesse, or we won't end up satisfying the second motive for doing it. Just about anything that hurts somebody else will satisfy the first motive for making us feel better. This, of course, only holds true for those of us who believe that inflicting pain on someone else will take away our own. However, it takes real creativity to come up with a humorous, not too nasty, yet slightly barbed way of getting even that sends just the right message to the other party without permanently damaging the relationship.

A friend once related a story to me about a male coworker in the engineering firm where she worked who kept sending her crude and unwanted love letters. This was in the era before sexual harassment was a widely visible issue, so any formal complaints she made were likely to be ignored or dismissed as trivial. But she came up with a simple solution. She walked up to him while he was in the midst of a conversation with his boss, smiled sweetly, handed him the stack of letters, and said, "I think you forgot these on my desk." After that, he left her alone.

Regina Barreca describes another sparkling comeback with such a touch. Liz Hamilton, who worked in the Johnson White House, had recently written a book and was approached by Arthur Schlesinger, Jr., at a cocktail party, who commented, "I liked your book, Liz. Who wrote it for you?" She said, "Glad you liked it, Arthur. Who read it to you?"

Most of us aren't that quick-witted. We stand tongue-tied as a difficult person emits various toxins, and only later do we think up just the right thing to say or do. But by the that time, it's too late.

The third motive for revenge is to prevent future harm. Some unpleasant people will continue their difficult behavior as long as they can get away with it. Revenge serves as a way to let them know that they will pay for any future transgressions.

However, when revenge is used as a preventive tactic, things can go wrong. Like medicine, revenge has side effects. First, it can escalate. When the target of a vengeful act decides to retaliate, this can lead to a cycle of growing ferocity. Several of the world's most intransigent conflicts, such as those in the Middle East and the Balkans, are based on repeated acts of vengeance that go back and forth through history.

Second, revenge can do permanent damage. A relationship scarred by an act of revenge may never recover. This is why some of the most ruthless acts of revenge are perpetrated upon those with whom one has no desire to ever interact again. Revenge is not exactly a recipe for rebuilding a relationship.

So, is revenge a viable course of action in our repertoire of potential responses to a difficult person? The answer depends on whether revenge offers the best way of satisfying each of the motives that inspire it. If our primary motive is to heal personal pain, there may be better ways than to add to the hurt already in this world. Later in this book I offer a number of approaches for dealing with the feelings that difficult people engender. In other words, if you're feeling bad, it may make you feel better to get even, but there are other ways to feel better that do less damage.

What if the primary motive is to send a message? This assumes one is skilled enough to devise a revenge strategy that has the desired effect of educating without burning bridges and being unduly harsh. Usually, one is too enraged during the plotting phase to think clearly about the ramifications of an act of revenge, and by the time one calms down to think it all through, the desire for revenge has calmed down as well. Even if one has the presence of mind to plot a suitable revenge, there is no guarantee the other person will get the message. Chances are, he will just think the avenger is an idiot. Revenge is not only an ineffective way of dealing with emotions, it's an inefficient way to communicate a message. It's indirect, it's invalidating, and it's one-way.

What about using revenge to deter appalling behavior from continuing? Should one fight back? The best choice here is, if possible, to bring in reinforcements by working through existing legal and societal channels instead of going after the person on your own. There are many established ways of responding to mistreatment. For example, at work you can go to the human resources department, or file a complaint with a government agency. In a private conflict, there is arbitration or the legal system.

Violence is never acceptable. As one example, consider someone who has been a victim of an assault. He has an absolute right to keep it from happening again, but his starting point should be the police, not retaliation. Reciprocal violence as an alternative is risky and dangerous. While agencies and courts may not always solve problems satisfactorily, mayhem creates many, many new ones.

The best way to view thoughts of revenge is as temptations to be resisted. It is psychologically healthy to entertain revenge fantasies, but they should remain as fantasies—once we do the deed, we have crossed a perilous line. When we feel a desire for revenge, we don't have to act on it. Instead, we can examine the desire to see what it reveals about ourselves. Why are we so enraged? How has our dignity been raped? What secret, shameful part of us is being revealed?

Our desire for revenge is a way to reclaim that part of ourselves that a difficult person has taken away. The nature of our fantasies will tell us what we want back. For example, when my dorm room was invaded and I was dumped in the shower, I felt powerless. My superglue fantasy was a way for me to feel powerful again by "jailing" my assailants.

Revenge fantasies are harmless. Revenge itself is a purely selfish act, done solely for one's own satisfaction. It may help a person to feel better, but at someone else's expense. Revenge does not promote sensitivity, communication, or caring. Nor does it contribute to building a better society—our system of jurisprudence was designed specifically to replace private acts of vengeance.

Perhaps the most useful way to get even is to use the feelings that difficult people stir up in you to understand yourself and make improvements in your life. When the neighborhood bully steals your son's lunch money, enroll together in a martial arts dojo. When a coworker bad-mouths you to higher-ups, take a night course and impress your boss with the latest Internet marketing techniques.

What George Herbert said in the seventeenth century still applies today:

Living well is the best revenge.

Getting a Difficult Person to Change: Not Very Likely

Be not angry that you cannot make others as you wish them to be since you cannot make yourself as you wish to be.

THOMAS À KEMPIS

An almost universal aspiration experienced by those dealing with difficult people is the desire to make them change what they are doing. We hope and pray that they will stop doing whatever it is that is driving us crazy. Or we fervently wish that they would start doing what we think they should be doing. This would surely make us feel better—just thinking about it brings relief.

Unfortunately, this kind of thinking places us in an undesirable predicament.

The problem is that we end up basing our well-being on someone else's behavior. This gives them enormous power over our state of mind. When they're nice, we're relieved. When they're difficult, we go bonkers. Our feelings are dictated by their behaviors, behaviors over which we have little or no control. At best we can make efforts to get them to change, and if they actually listen and do something, we feel good. But most of the time this good feeling is only temporary because people often revert to their old ways, and we're back where we started.

If you've ever tried to make a change in your own behavior, you will know instantly why difficult people can't be expected to change. Even when you are highly motivated yourself, change doesn't always stick. Now imagine someone who's being difficult. What's in it for them?

To effectively deal with a difficult person, we need to accept the fact that getting that person to change may not be a realistic goal.

Getting a Difficult Person to Change: Still Worth a Try

Nothing so needs reforming as other people's habits.

MARK TWAIN

Let's set aside our pessimism about changing others for a moment and assume that it is indeed possible to get someone else to change. After all, it does happen. Some people with drinking problems do stop; some people who criticize others do refrain; some people who have volatile tempers do manage to control themselves.

Why do some people change while others don't? Why do our efforts succeed with some people while others just go on doing what they've been doing? Personal change has three elements: awareness, willingness, and ability.

First, a person must be aware that his behavior is causing problems for someone else. If he isn't, it's a given that he'll keep doing what he's been doing. For example, the fact that your secretary spends all day making personal calls may make you furious, but if he doesn't think he's doing anything wrong, and you don't speak up, he's going to continue.

Second, a person has to want to change. People who are difficult will only change if it's in their best interest; otherwise, they won't. Why should they? Change requires a lot of motivation; old habits aren't easily overcome. There needs to be some sort of payoff for people to actually make the necessary effort. They have to care enough to make the change because the relationship matters to them. Or they have to want to change because the benefits of changing clearly outweigh the penalties for not changing. Your daughter is not going to suddenly start cleaning up her room just because you ask unless there are rewards or consequences.

Third, a person has to be able to change. In an ideal world, everyone who wants to could make changes that needed to be made. But in the world we live in, some people just can't change, even when they try. Dieters do regain weight, recovering alcoholics can start to drink again, and people with bad tempers do tend to lose them even after a period of self-control.

How then can we get others to change? There are several approaches at our disposal: power, influence, and love. Let's explore each in turn.

It is possible to get someone to change, but we need to know what we're doing and whether the other person is likely to be receptive to our efforts.

Change, or Else!

You see what power is—holding someone else's fear in your hand and showing it to them!

AMY TAN

Power is the ability to get someone else to do something that she wouldn't do otherwise. In order to do so, one needs only to acquire a source of power.

One such source is money, or alternately, the ability to reward. For the right price, I should be able to get you to act in ways that satisfy me. If I have something you need, and I'm willing to give it to you if you agree to certain conditions, that gives me power over you.

Another source of power is the ability to punish. Fear works quite well as a means to get others to do what we want. Of course, invoking fear in our interpersonal relationships doesn't exactly foster cordial relations.

Another source of power comes from one's position. A boss, parent, priest, or teacher automatically has the right to tell someone what do so as long as the directives fall within the confines of a predefined relationship. Outside the relationship, power ceases to exist. A priest can't tell a Muslim how to repent; a parent can't discipline the next-door neighbor.

One also holds power if one has expertise. When your doctor tells you to take your clothes off, you comply because you want something he or she has—medical knowledge.

Charisma often brings power. If you respect, admire, and revere someone, you are more inclined to do what that person asks. Some people spend much of their lives devoted to a cause solely because of their feelings toward the person who espouses it. That's why so many cults continue to thrive.

So, the solution to dealing with difficult people would appear to be simple. Acquire power over them. That, in fact, is what many people attempt to do throughout their lives. They quest after power and try to make others do their bidding. They acquire wealth or use intimidation to control others.

Becoming powerful does eliminate some of life's annoyances. But it also creates new problems.

It is isolating to have relationships with others based only on one's power over them; we've all heard the expression, "It's lonely at the top." No one I know likes being forced to do something; a person might comply out of necessity but won't have fond feelings for whoever wields the power. In other words, power will work to get someone to change as long as you don't care what the other person thinks or feels about you.

More dangerous is what can happen to those who seek power for personal reasons and lack the maturity to use it wisely. Unless power is used in conjunction with wisdom to further not just personal goals but the welfare of others, it invariably corrupts the person who uses it. Power is necessary to get things done; but when power is used instead to satisfy personal needs, it has the tendency to bring out our baser instincts and less admirable qualities. When external sources of power are sought in personal relationships to overcome inner feelings of powerlessness, power comes not from a place of strength but from a place of weakness. This can only lead to trouble.

> **Using power to deal with difficult people is like driving your car over a pile of walnuts to crack them open. Both might work, but that's not what they were designed to do.**

Let's Make a Deal

> *Let us never negotiate out of fear, but let us never fear to negotiate.*
>
> JOHN F. KENNEDY

Influence, our second approach to getting someone to change, involves the other person's agreement. When we use power over others, we are forcing change; when we use influence, we are requesting it. There are many influence strategies we can use in our daily interactions.

As an illustration, imagine that you are grieving the recent loss of a close friend and coworker who has just died of lung cancer. Now you are more concerned than ever about your sister, who continues to smoke heavily. You'd like to influence her to stop.

One way that we influence people is by using facts and logic. You might try to get your sister to stop smoking by reminding her about the health hazards. Or you could point out that she'll have a harder time finding a new job, since some employers are less likely to hire smokers.

Another way you might try to influence her is by negotiating or bargaining. You might offer to treat your sister to a vacation in the Caribbean if she quits for at least six months, or promise you'll go on a diet as part of the deal.

A third way that we influence people is through the use of threats. You might tell your sister that she is no longer welcome in your house if she continues to smoke, or warn her that you will continue to nag her about the issue every time you see her until she promises to stop.

In contrast, we also use friendliness and warmth to influence. You could tell your sister you care about her and that you're concerned about her health.

Sometimes we influence people by joining forces with others to make our impact stronger. Before the next family get-together, you might call everyone in advance and plan a group confrontation after dinner.

Invoking guilt is a classic influence strategy. You could tell your sister how much your mother worries about her and how your nieces will suffer if their mother dies prematurely.

Sometimes we try to influence people indirectly. You might call the local chapter of the cancer society and ask them to send your sister literature, or mention how upset you are about your friend's death without bringing up the subject of your sister's smoking.

One can also be direct. You could just tell your sister that you'd like to see her stop, or ask her to smoke outside whenever she comes over, without using guilt, threats, hints, deals, help from others, or factual arguments.

These examples are far from complete, but they do give you the range of possibilities.

With all these choices, how *does* one know which to use? When is a particular influence strategy most likely to work?

As a starting point, it is useful to recognize that influence strategies are rarely chosen deliberately and consciously, as the previous discussion might imply. They tend instead to emerge spontaneously and without forethought.

While preparing to write this book, I spent time researching other books on the subject of dealing with difficult people. Almost all of them advocate a similar approach—they offer specific suggestions for selecting the particular influence strategy that is most likely to be effective in dealing with a particular type of difficult person. The books present lists of difficult types. One then identifies the type that best describes the situation at hand. For each type, there are recommendations for dealing with the person and suggestions for saying the right thing.

If using one-time psychological techniques and someone else's words to deal with a specific situation is appealing to you, then books of this type can be useful. But formulas like these aren't very effective over time, because each of us has our own style and preference for influencing others. We tend to first use what worked for us growing up. As a child, if we wanted something from our parents or other grown-ups, we learned that saying things a certain way got us what we wanted. As adults, out of habit and due to unconscious patterns, we may continue trying tactics that used to work. When they don't, we act surprised and disappointed.

Before we can be effective at influencing others, we need to understand what our preferred style is and learn how to use other styles when appropriate.

Using ineffective influence tactics has been an embarrassing trait in my own life. I had a tendency that was hard for me to shake in which I persisted to the point of annoyance when I wanted something from someone with whom I was close. I didn't give up easily—I kept asking until I got a firm no or the other party gave in. It worked quite well when I was a kid. However, when my perseverance (described by those close to me in less complimentary terms) didn't produce the effect I hoped for, I got frustrated with the other person and failed to recognize, at least initially, that *I* was the source of the problem.

Sometimes we label someone as difficult not because of what he does to us but because our influence attempts aren't working. He seems difficult because we want a yes that he won't give us. It is easy to overlook our own ineffective contribution to the difficulties.

In addition to being an ineffectual influencer, I've also been at the receiving end of all kinds of oafish influence tactics. One is especially memorable. When I was in my twenties, I worked with someone in a nonprofit organization who hammered away at my self-esteem when he wanted something from me. He belittled me and tried to make me feel like dirt anytime I took a stance that stymied his. Unfortunately, I wasn't astute enough then to figure out how to let him know that his behavior was unacceptable and to prevent his tactic from working on me. It usually worked on others as well, because people would say yes just to get him to shut up. He got what he wanted, but at the price of no one liking or respecting him.

Some influence attempts work, and some don't. But what does it mean when we say that an influence attempt is working?

Does it just mean that we are getting what we want, or are there other considerations?

There are actually two ways of looking at what works. A particular way of influencing others might or might not get us what we want. At the same time, and this is usually not as apparent to us, our way of influencing the other person might maintain the relationship, or it might alienate the other person. The trick, as you may surmise, is to find an approach that both gets us what we want and takes the other person's feelings and concerns into consideration.

Looking back at the list of ways you might get your sister to stop smoking, some might work and some probably won't. At the same time, some would improve your relationship with your sister, while others would do it harm.

In general, being direct and reasonable works better than being indirect and unreasonable. People prefer logical approaches, honesty, and negotiations; they dislike threats, manipulation, hints, and deceit. At the core of any successful influence attempt is the requirement to respect and show interest in the other person's needs and concerns without sacrificing your own. In chapter 6 we'll explore some of the ways that difficult people can be effectively influenced so that our needs and concerns receive a receptive airing and we don't cause further damage to an already problematic relationship.

To summarize our consideration of influence as a way of changing a difficult person—it works just fine if you know what you're doing.

Influence is a skill that needs to be learned, and like any skill, whether it be bowling or lovemaking, some of us are better at it than others. Influencing people we are on good terms with isn't always easy; influencing difficult people effectively is a true art.

The Transforming Power of Love

Love is the only force capable of transforming an enemy into a friend.

MARTIN LUTHER KING, JR.

Love is our third approach to changing others. It is the most powerful, the most healing, and the most transformational. It is also the hardest to use. The Bible tells us to love our enemies, but it doesn't tell us how. It takes an extraordinary person to express love to someone who continually makes them miserable.

Stories of difficult people transformed by the power of love have been a popular literary theme throughout history. There are any number of movies in which a person of troublesome character softens under the influence of someone's love. Reading about and watching these conversions of the heart touch something deep within us.

Even though love is the most potent way to influence another, it cannot just be acquired through techniques, practices, or advice. A loving heart is cultivated, often over a period of years. It is a state of being, and is attained through steady effort.

If you can find a place in your heart to love someone regardless of what they do, you are blessed. There is no better way in Creation to heal the difficulties between you.

Changing Yourself

A person should realize that conflict situations between oneself and others are nothing but the effects of conflict situations in one's own soul.

MARTIN BUBER

Let's review what we've considered so far in our choices about how to deal with a difficult person. We've seen that doing nothing just perpetuates the problem. Making nice works only in the short term. Leaving is disruptive and should be chosen only as a last resort when other options haven't proven successful. Getting even might help you feel better, but it is essentially a selfish act that sabotages future relations. Trying to foster successful and lasting change in another person requires skill and finesse.

So now we come to our final option: changing ourselves. If we ponder for a moment, we'll realize that this is the only way to have total control over the results of our efforts. It is not possible to successfully predict and influence how another will act. It is possible, however, for us to influence how *we* act.

At first glance, changing our response to a difficult person is deceptively easy. All we have to do is stop reacting to the other person. That's right. Just let go of the feelings you're having about the whole thing, and don't let the situation annoy you anymore.

To truly let go is a very liberating experience. But letting go is something few people can do, because emotions are spontaneous; one can't just switch them on and off. People who do appear to be able to turn off their feelings may just be repressing them, which has unhealthy consequences. Furthermore, pretending that we don't care when we really do is just self-deception. It doesn't work.

So if we can't just make our feelings go away, what does it mean to change ourselves?

Fundamentally, changing ourselves starts with our feelings. Most of our responses to difficult people are emotional; what we say and do is almost always related to managing unpleasant feelings, whether or not we realize it. If we pay attention to our feelings, we have an additional source of information about our difficulties. And if we have learned to work with our feelings instead of resisting them, then we can respond more appropriately. We always struggle more with our own emotions than we actually struggle with another person.

To change ourselves we also have to change our perspective and way of seeing difficulties. We can derive great benefit if we reframe the situation and view it as an opportunity to learn about ourselves and become better persons. Changing our perspective means using the situation to recognize and work on our own shortcomings instead of focusing on the other person's.

Finally, if this universe we inhabit isn't just a random series of events and there is purpose to this life we live, then to change ourselves also means to look for spiritual meaning in our suffering. In the next two chapters we'll learn how to view our difficulties through a spiritual lens and focus the light so that we can use our struggles to grow a little closer to the divine.

Many books contain specific techniques for dealing with difficult people. They tell you what to say and do in specific situations. This is not one of them. My goal is not to teach you tricks to use in the moment but to foster inner change as a lasting foundation for all your interpersonal encounters. If, as this book maintains, the people in your life are there to help you with your spiritual development, then what you really need is not coaching in what to say to a difficult person but help in working on yourself and seeing the spiritual meaning behind your difficulties.

The most powerful option for dealing with a difficult person is personal growth. Inner change inevitably leads to outer change.

Explorations

STRATEGIES FOR DEALING WITH DIFFICULT PEOPLE

Purpose: To identify your primary method of responding to difficult people

Each of us has a tendency to respond to difficult people in a particular way. Think back to your last few encounters with difficult people. What did you do?

- Did you avoid dealing with the problem or pretend everything was fine?
- Did you make nice and actively try to please the other person?
- Did you think about leaving or actually leave?
- Did you think about getting even or engaging in revenge?
- Did you fight back through institutional or legal avenues?
- Did you try to change what the other person was doing?
- Did you ask yourself what you could be learning from the situation?

As we discussed earlier in this chapter, each approach has its advantages and disadvantages. If you have a tendency to rely on a particular option, consider whether the option is the one that serves you best.

CHAPTER 3

WHY ARE PEOPLE DIFFICULT?

Knowing the Enemy

The first rule of war: know your enemy.

SAM KEEN

As I write this on a cold New England morning in mid-January, two teams are assiduously preparing for the upcoming Super Bowl by studying videos of the opposition. And a recent bizarre murder is receiving national media attention while FBI experts put forth psychological profiles of the slayer.

Not just in January, but throughout the year, lawyers across the nation keep busy developing legal strategies for forthcoming trials by painstakingly analyzing the opposing side. Market researchers in corporate offices dissect the latest product of their competitor to find ways of entering the marketplace with a better one. And in undisclosed, nondescript places, highly trained intelligence analysts study satellite surveillance photographs of nations that might pose a threat to national interests or the security of allies.

All these diverse efforts have one goal—to better understand an adversary.

In the previous chapter, we considered different options for dealing with difficult people. Yet our capacity to choose the most effective option depends in large part on whom we are dealing with in the first place. So an understanding of difficult people is essential if we are to successfully resolve our problems.

In this chapter, we examine various reasons why people are difficult. Our twin goals are to resolve our present difficulties and to prevent future ones. In our examination, we'll consider whether the difficulties are due to the situation or the person, and we'll assess the difficult person's degree of responsibility.

To deal with a difficult person, you need to know just whom you're dealing with and why that person acts that way.

Some Difficult People Aren't

My duty is to obey orders.

STONEWALL JACKSON

If you were to ask Roger, a divorce attorney, about the most difficult person in his life, he would immediately mention David, the lawyer representing his client's husband in a protracted and often nasty divorce proceeding. These two attorneys were constantly arguing and filing new motions. Roger had never encountered anyone as tenacious and unyielding as his opponent. He was obsessed with besting him and getting the best settlement.

One weekend, the two attorneys happened to bump into each other in a shopping mall with their children in tow. Surprised to see each other out of court and clientless, they exchanged cautious greetings. Roger found David unexpectedly friendly and reasonable, totally unlike his courtroom persona. As they watched their children play by a fountain, they let down their guard and exchanged thoughts. David, it turned out, was just doing his job. His client was the difficult one. The client wanted to come out ahead in the divorce proceedings at all costs; the unreasonableness and nastiness in the courtroom that David exhibited were expected by the client as part of the process. David didn't like acting that way, but his client demanded it, and if he wanted to keep the client, he had to perform according to the client's requests.

Reasonable people in unreasonable circumstances can appear to be difficult. But they may just be responding to the realities of their situation, which demands certain behaviors. If we take the time to understand their position, we will often find that we would have done the same if we were under the same external pressures.

Some difficult people aren't; they are just caught up in a situation or role that requires them to act in a certain way.

Some People Are Different, Not Difficult

Differences were meant by God not to divide but to enrich.

J. H. OLDHAM

Elizabeth, who worked in an important state government position in the Midwest, received a special award from the governor's office for outstanding service. She deserved it. She was impeccably organized, willing to put in extra hours, on time with deadlines, and helpful to coworkers and the public. In her personal life as well, she was loved and respected by her friends and family. She rarely forgot a birthday and seldom failed to send a prompt thank-you note for any kindness. She served on a number of civic and religious committees, was the embodiment of responsibility and thoughtfulness, and was utterly dependable.

But there was one problem. She thought highly of herself and her competence, and she expected everyone else to be like her and live life by her standards. So when someone failed to acknowledge her birthday, or missed a deadline, or had a messy office, she was critical and sometimes made caustic remarks.

Elizabeth saw other people in her life as difficult when the reality was that they were just different.

Many of us go through life wondering what's wrong with other people. We judge others by our own standards; we apply our view of reality to their lives and find them lacking. We admire traits in others that we admire in ourselves; we denigrate others when their behavior doesn't conform to our values. We find it almost impossible to climb inside someone else's head and see the world through different eyes.

People are different. People differ in temperament and values and personality; they have different talents, different interests, different goals. They are not always acting difficult when we think they are; they are just being true to themselves. They see the world differently than we do, stemming from the values taught in their family of origin, their life histories, their cultural and religious backgrounds, and their genetic inheritance.

Some people are viewed as difficult because they are not like us. We fail to appreciate that they see the world differently than we do and their perspective is just as legitimate as ours.

Some Difficult People Just Don't Have a Clue

It is worse still to be ignorant of your ignorance.

SAINT JEROME

Some years ago, a friend I'll call Bob regularly walked right into the house I lived in without knocking. The habit continued even after I asked him several times to stop. Bob was annoying and invasive, and he just didn't have a clue that it was inappropriate to barge in on people.

Nevertheless, the friendship somehow survived, and at some

later point, I ended up visiting his boyhood home. When I saw Bob's childhood bedroom, I noticed it didn't have a door. At that moment, something inside clicked. I suddenly understood his inability to appreciate other people's need for privacy. Growing up, Bob didn't have any.

There are two mechanisms in society that educate us. The first is schooling. If we attend substandard schools or fail to acquire enough education, our future income and career options suffer.

The second mechanism is our family. If we grow up in a dysfunctional family, our social skills suffer, and we fail to learn appropriate ways of interacting with others.

The most probable explanation for someone being difficult is that no one ever taught them the basics. They are clueless and because of their history have a hard time learning the behaviors that most people take for granted.

When facing someone else's perplexing behavior, it may be helpful to consider the possibility that the person may not know any better. Appropriate behaviors that are obvious to you may not be so obvious to someone else.

Some Difficult People Are Stuck in the Past

Our daughters and sons have burst
from the marionette show
leaving a tangle of strings
and gone into the unlit audience.

MAXINE KUMIN

Imagine for a moment that you have not one but two bosses at work. The bosses don't always agree with each other and sometimes give you conflicting assignments. You usually end up spending more time taking orders from one of them; the other shows up from time to time but doesn't seem to know what's going on. There is lots to complain about at work—you are often asked to do ridiculous things, and you are never taken seriously. There are small annoyances—the bathrooms are seldom clean, the coffee always runs out, your chair is uncomfortable. Yet when you express displeasure both verbally and nonverbally, your bosses never seem to get the message clearly. It's as if they don't understand the language you speak. They listen as if they're interested, they might check on you and fix something for a while, but essentially they just keep on doing whatever they've been doing. And when visitors from other companies show up from time to time, they're even worse—they do annoying things, pay far too much attention to you, and you can't wait for them to leave. However, the pay and benefits are excellent considering how little work you actually do, so at least this part of your situation is good. On the other hand, because of a unique contract, you can't work anywhere else.

Every single one of us has "worked" under these circumstances, whether they appear familiar or not. The bosses mirror our parents, and the working conditions reflect our early childhood.

As infants and young children, we are strongly influenced by our environment since we are both highly impressionable and completely powerless. Our childhood influences us so strongly that the types of relationships that we have then influence all our subsequent relationships throughout life.

Much of clinical psychology and psychiatry consists of analyzing how these early relationships with parents, siblings, and caregivers affect us in the present, a concept called transference. For a lucky few, the initial influences were loving, nurturing, and healthy. These people don't have many unresolved issues about their childhood; when they meet new people, the past doesn't tend to intrude on the present and they are able to see others more or less as they are.

But for many, much remains unresolved; when they interact with someone, they have a tendency to unconsciously see the person as a reflection of someone in their past rather than as a unique individual.

So another reason that people are difficult is because they are stuck—they relate to you as if you were someone else. It is as if you have unknowingly become a player in a complex drama of their making, with a role you don't comprehend.

Some years ago a very likable man named Joel joined the company where I worked. Joel was eager to please and possessed a lot of personal charm. Initially we got along well. But not too long after starting the job, Joel began making questionable decisions.

When I tried to discuss these decisions with him, Joel didn't react as a typical employee might. His behavior toward me shifted, and I suddenly turned into an adversary. He no longer paid attention to my opinion or consulted me on work matters. He was convinced that I was wrong and he was right.

I soon realized these shifts in behavior weren't just happening to me. Systematically, he was alienating every single male at work who disagreed with his decisions while turning to the women in the office to commiserate about all the men who didn't understand him. Under pressure, he soon left the company, and I subsequently learned he had left his previous job under similar circumstances.

Joel had grown up with a father who disliked him and criticized everything he did. Joel turned to his mother for solace and comfort as a way to ease the pain of his father's constant onslaught.

In adulthood, Joel re-created this childhood pattern wherever he went. As soon as someone criticized him, that person turned into his father. And the women in his life served as surrogate mothers, providing the emotional support he desperately sought.

I gleaned several useful insights from this experience with Joel. The first is that when someone is being difficult, it isn't necessarily about me—I don't always have to take things personally when a relationship becomes problematic. Joel would have had a problem with anyone who disagreed with him—I just happened to be there.

The second insight I had was the recognition that when I find someone difficult, I could be the one who is stuck in the past, not the other person. Joel eventually saw all his coworkers as enemies, failing to recognize the role his own history played. To Joel, everyone at work was a difficult person. However, if it could happen to Joel, it could also happen to me. I am not immune to making the same errors. Now, when I find someone difficult, I try to ask myself whether the person is triggering old feelings by reminding me of a difficult person in my own distant past.

When someone is being difficult, two things could be happening. You could be reminding her of a difficult person in her past, or she could be reminding you of a difficult person in your past.

Some Difficult People Are in Emotional Kindergarten

People who cannot feel punish those who do.

MAY SARTON

Grant was very proud of the software business he had built, which combined his MBA in finance with years of computer wizardry. His sophisticated knowledge enabled him to continuously develop new products to meet the specialized needs of his East Coast banking and financial service customers. Now that his business had grown rapidly, most of his former routine contacts with these customers had to be delegated to his staff since he couldn't be everywhere at once.

The problem was that no one could do the job well enough. Those with offices down the hall from Grant would periodically hear him screaming at employees for their supposed incompetence in handling customers. Those who weren't fired ended up quitting, disgusted by his abusive treatment. As a result, business began to suffer.

Grant may have earned his master's degree, but emotionally he was still in kindergarten. He could not manage his own emotions and was utterly insensitive to the ways he impacted others.

In the book *Emotional Intelligence,* Daniel Goleman describes the qualities of those who have emotional mastery:

- They are able to recognize a feeling as it arises; this gives them a greater sense of the "rightness" of the decisions they make, since they are in tune with an additional way of knowing besides their intellect.
- They are able to manage their emotional reactions when debilitating emotions dominate.
- They are able to use their emotions appropriately in pursuit of a goal by delaying gratification and stifling impulsiveness.
- They are sensitive to the feelings of others.
- They are able to skillfully work with and influence others' emotional states to build and strengthen personal relationships.

Most people are difficult because they lack one or more of these qualities; those like Grant who appear to be emotionally handicapped in their interactions with others are especially troublesome.

Some people are difficult because they lack basic emotional awareness and skills.

Some Difficult People Have Emotional Wounds

Deep in her breast lives the silent wound.

VIRGIL

Suzanne had a bad year. First, she lost her job. Then she miscarried several times, her feelings of grief spiraling at each loss. When her grandmother also died, she fell into a deep well of sorrow.

As a little girl, when Suzanne would visit her grandmother, she was always gently covered with a quilt during her naps. The quilt had a wonderful, indescribable scent, and it held warm, comforting memories. So when she asked her aunt, the executor of her grandmother's estate, if she could have the quilt, it was a request not just for a keepsake but for a blanket of love to help heal all her losses.

Her aunt said no. Suzanne reacted with the full measure of her pain. She screamed. She said terrible things to her aunt. She cried for a very long time.

An outside observer who didn't know Suzanne's story might say that Suzanne overreacted to her aunt and was being difficult and unreasonable. Suzanne, on the other hand, saw her aunt as the unreasonable one, since she had denied a simple request and ignored the impact of Suzanne's sorrowful year.

Suzanne was so filled with grief that she reacted completely out of proportion to the circumstance. It was as if someone had slapped her on the back without realizing she had a severe sunburn.

Some people, like Suzanne, react the way they do because of emotional wounds caused by recent events. But many emotional wounds go back to childhood and operate unconsciously. These wounds can cause someone to overreact to actions that are ordinarily harmless. People will go to great lengths to avoid experiencing the emotions associated with old wounds.

Difficult people aren't the only ones who carry emotional wounds. We all do. One of the reasons difficult people get to us is that they trigger our own deeply buried wounds from the past.

Some people are difficult because they are emotionally wounded. The way that we respond emotionally to difficult people shows us our own emotional wounds, revealing the places inside that need healing.

Some Difficult People Have Low Self-Esteem

A man cannot be comfortable without his own approval.

MARK TWAIN

Steve didn't like himself very much. He wasn't athletic growing up, so he wasn't very popular as a boy. In high school, a severe acne problem made him a target for classmates to taunt and ridicule with cruel put-downs. He learned to respond in kind with nasty comments of his own. The acne eventually healed, but the emotional scars stayed.

Luckily, Steve was smart. He excelled in college at his chosen field, engineering, and went on to earn an advanced degree in packaging. He rose quickly at his job with a large corporation, designing machinery to package various food products.

By this time, Steve's facility at verbal assault equaled his technical expertise. Coworkers stayed clear so they wouldn't become targets for his sarcasm and subtle insults. If he felt attacked, he let loose with a devastating barrage. Steve's sense of self was so fragile he needed to protect it by keeping people at a distance.

Some difficult behaviors are the result of low self-esteem, a particularly devastating type of emotional wound. People who don't like themselves have various ways of interacting with the world to prevent themselves from being hurt again.

Some people with low self-esteem, like Steve, use words as a defense. Others may just keep to themselves, preferring loneliness to the risk of rejection. Some crave sympathy and attention, constantly and annoyingly seeking an ear to listen or a shoulder to cry on. Others maintain an artificial facade while never revealing who they are, since to do so would be to allow for the possibility of their real self being rejected.

Some people are difficult because they don't like themselves and have devised various strategies to keep from being hurt again.

Nobody Knows the Troubles They've Seen

Great souls suffer in silence.
JOHANN CHRISTOPH FRIEDRICH VON SCHILLER

During the eight years I spent as a college professor, I heard every student excuse imaginable, from "the dog ate my disk" to "I had a job interview . . . at the beach." Over the years I found myself becoming increasingly skeptical with each new ruse and became less and less willing to believe them.

But sometimes, when I could get past my cynicism, I would discover that a paper hadn't been written or a test had been missed because of genuine hardship. One older student lost a son to illness. An undergraduate lost a beloved grandparent. Another's girlfriend was hospitalized in critical condition after a serious auto accident.

Some people are very public about tragedy, while others keep their suffering quiet. Some people manage to get through each day without any outward signs of their personal affliction. Others become difficult toward others as an unthinking response to their private anguish.

We have very little knowledge of what really goes on in the lives of others. An acquaintance of ours could have financial difficulties, a serious illness, or a family member with a drug problem that we could be completely unaware of.

Consider the possibility that someone is being difficult not just because he is having a bad day, but because he is having a bad life.

The Difficult Believer

Every form of addiction is bad, no matter whether the narcotic be alcohol or morphine or idealism.

C. G. JUNG

Some people are difficult because of the beliefs, ideals, and values they hold. What we see as stubborn and dogmatic behavior, they see as being noble and true to a greater cause.

Beliefs help us find certainty in an uncertain world. They provide us with points of reference for interpreting the unexpected. They sustain us and give us a reason to persist in the face of obstacles, resistance, and opposition. They offer a sense of community among those who share them.

At the same time, beliefs limit us. They inhibit our capacity to experience life's events in fresh, new ways. Beliefs also divide and separate. They create a believer/nonbeliever mentality that is used as justification for all sorts of difficult behaviors.

For example, we find public figures who decry and condemn those whose political beliefs differ from theirs, attacking the person, not just the posture. Religious leaders depict those who don't share their beliefs in the most unloving ways, failing to recognize that loving one's neighbor is one of the most meaningful ways to affirm one's faith.

People who cleave to their beliefs at the expense of others are more comfortable having relationships with ideas than with people. It's a lot easier. What they fail to recognize is that it's a lot lonelier.

It can be helpful to realize that some people are difficult because they need to hold tightly to their beliefs to feel comfortable and secure.

Some Difficult People Want Too Much

Short is the way from need to greed.

ABRAHAM JOSHUA HESCHEL

Wherever I turn, I am accosted with enticing advertisements. Highly paid and highly sophisticated ad agencies employ all their creative talents to influence my buying habits. I am exhorted to buy things I may not want and probably don't need with the promise that I will be sexier or healthier or have more fun.

There is no campaign with comparable volume that influences me to be kind and compassionate and loving, or to act in moderation, or to give generously to those in need. The loudest, most visible message I get every day from the society I live in is that I need to acquire to be happy. If I want to live my life according to a different, more spiritually based message, I have to seek that message out; it is almost imperceptible.

So it shouldn't be the least bit surprising that some people are strongly influenced by the ubiquitous religion of consumerism and faithfully attend its temple, the shopping mall, each Sabbath. They believe that acquiring more possessions will somehow provide them with what they lack.

Some people are difficult because they value things over people. When the desire for things goes beyond what is needed or necessary, it's called greed.

Wanting too much wouldn't cause problems in relationships if the effects were only confined to the person doing the wanting. Unfortunately, they aren't. Whenever someone wants too much, it is almost always at the expense of someone else. When a person is greedy, other people in his life tend to be viewed as objects to help him acquire what he seeks.

This trait is particularly prevalent in the business world, where the drive for profit can overwhelm any sense of responsibility to treat people with fairness and respect. Many of my MBA students as well as participants in my consulting programs have shared stories of bosses and business owners who saw them not as people but only as a means to make more money. In large corporations, if those at the top want too much, thousands of people may lose their livelihood in a layoff or plant closure, not because the business that employs them isn't profitable, but because the profit figures just aren't big enough.

Money and possessions aren't the only objects of greed. People can be greedy for power, or for status, or for fame. One might think of jealousy as greed for a particular person. Greed targets anything that shows promise of bestowing an enhanced sense of self. By acquiring something desirable, whether it be a luxury car, an expensive dress, or a prominent position, people feel better about themselves. But when the quest to elevate one's sense of self through the acquisition of something external gets out of balance, it can lead to the mistreatment of others. If someone feels she absolutely needs something outside herself to feel good, then acquiring whatever it is she needs will be her first priority in life. Other people are then viewed as helpers or obstacles; those who can assist in achieving her aim or those who get in the way. What others might think or feel or need becomes irrelevant in this single-minded quest.

Some people are uncaring and difficult because they view other people only as a means to their self-centered ends.

Some Difficult People Are Substance Abusers

Drunkenness spoils health, dismounts the mind, and unmans man. It reveals secrets, is quarrelsome, lascivious, impudent, dangerous and mad.

WILLIAM PENN

Alcohol is the most widely used drug in the world. It has been estimated that approximately 13 percent of adults have a problem with alcohol abuse or dependence during their lives, and that at least 5 percent are active alcoholics. In light of these statistics, one can assume that alcohol abuse explains the behavior of at least some difficult people. Among certain age, ethnic, and cultural groups, the percentage of those who abuse alcohol is likely to be even higher.

Those who abuse alcohol tend to be anxious, irritable, and impatient, even when alcohol has not been ingested. Intoxication can lead to aggression, intense mood swings, poor judgment, and impaired social functioning. At least half of traffic fatalities and homicides and a quarter of suicides are linked to alcohol.

For anyone whose life has been affected by alcohol, this information is not news.

Other drugs besides alcohol have marked effects on behavior. Barbiturate use can lead to hostility, quarrelsomeness, moroseness, and paranoia. Heroin use generates lethargy and drowsiness; during periods of withdrawal, users experience anxiety and agitation. Amphetamine abuse and high doses of cocaine, which is considered the most addictive drug, may result in impaired social functioning, aggression, and extreme agitation. Hallucinogens such as LSD can create intense emotional experiences, illusions, and hallucinations. Marijuana use can lead to suspiciousness and slowed reaction time.

An addiction to any one of these drugs can foment criminal behavior if the addict desperately needs to support his or her habit.

This is a sobering list.

Simply put, people with substance abuse problems need help. Some realize that they do, and some don't. It is very unlikely that relationship difficulties with a substance abuser will begin to be resolved until after the person stops using. For your own sanity, if your life is linked up with someone who is a substance abuser, seriously consider attending twelve-step meetings in a program such as Al-Anon.

Some people are difficult because they abuse alcohol or drugs. Difficulties with a substance abuser will continue until the person seeks help and stops using and/or abusing.

Some Difficult People Are Mentally Ill

Any man who goes to a psychiatrist should have his head examined.

SAM GOLDWYN

I admit to being a self-improvement junkie, one of my qualifications for writing this book. I read self-help books, meditate, attend therapy, take classes, go on retreats, and "work on my own stuff" with varying degrees of insight, success, and silliness. I make an effort not to take things too seriously, not to be too earnest or obnoxious or obsessive. I avoid the jargon of the week.

It's my hobby. I find it a fascinating one, since there is always something new to learn and always new avenues for exploration.

That's why it amazes me on the rare occasions when I meet someone who claims there is nothing wrong with him and no need for him to pursue personal improvement.

At its extreme, this kind of denial is a form of mental illness. A person's behavior may vary considerably from accepted norms, but that person will still insist that he's fine. When reality rudely intrudes in the form of feedback from a concerned friend or family member, it is unwelcome.

Once, when I lived in Minnesota and my neighbors upstairs went on vacation, they had an acquaintance house-sit in their absence. She wore elegant clothes, drove an expensive and exotic foreign car, and was broke because she couldn't keep a job. I helped her bring her luggage up the stairs. Upon arriving, she pulled down all the shades because the sunlight bothered her eyes. She was thin and had a strange curl to her fingers. Her speech was ethereal, odd, and halting. It was apparent to me and anyone else who met her that she had a problem.

When my friends returned, I expressed concern and described what had gone on. They gently suggested to her that she might want to seek help. She recoiled angrily and never spoke to them again.

Some people are difficult because they suffer from a serious mental disorder. They need help but may not realize it or want to admit it. I've heard it said that the main difference between those who seek psychological help and those who don't is that the first group is healthier. At least they're willing to do something about their problems.

Mental disorders come in a variety of forms, too numerous to describe. Some have organic origins, meaning there is an identifiable, physiological cause. Others have their origins in childhood, or current stress, or simply genetic inheritance. Many are treatable with medication. Some problems benefit greatly from therapy.

Getting a difficult person to recognize he or she needs help is a delicate process. Ironically, if you are the person suffering the most from a difficult person with a mental disorder, your advice is probably the least credible. In that person's mind, *you* may be the source of the difficulties.

If a person is difficult because of a mental disorder, that person needs help. As in the case of substance abusers, relationship difficulties are unlikely to improve until the difficult person's mental status improves.

Sick and Tired

Your father's sickness is a maim to us.
WILLIAM SHAKESPEARE (*Henry IV, Part One*)

Sometimes people who are normally easy to deal with become difficult when they are tired or ill. The person is not inherently difficult, just being a temporary pain.

Nevertheless, someone who is being a temporary pain can still be temporarily painful. A friend once related to me a long litany of trying experiences he suffered while caring for his elderly mother, who was bedridden and seriously ill. She would periodically make sharp comments that left him hurt and resentful. Nurses wouldn't stay because of her abusive treatment. In truth, she was terrified of dying and utterly unable to cope with her incapacity after having lived a vigorous life. To deal with these feelings, she lashed out at everyone.

Sometimes the effect of illness is less direct but no less difficult. Katia, an energetic and busy mother of two involved in many community activities, was felled by an unusual form of food poisoning called ciguatera. Ciguatera is a toxin produced by plankton that grow on tropical reefs in the Caribbean. Smaller fish eat the plankton along with the toxin, and then larger fish eat the smaller fish. Katia had dined on red snapper while on vacation in the West Indies on the island of Saint Martin. Within an hour, she found herself extremely fatigued at the slightest effort. In addition, she began to suffer from severe joint pain and a bizarre hypersensitivity to cold on her palms, the soles of her feet, and inside her mouth.

When she returned home she was practically bedridden and unable to do anything around the house. Her family, accustomed to her constant support, had to learn a whole new way of functioning without her. She wasn't being difficult to anyone, but the circumstances became extremely trying for her family. It was as if they were dealing with a difficult person who wasn't there.

Sometimes people are difficult or situations are made difficult by illness or fatigue.

With Malice Toward Some

Wisdom entereth not into a malicious mind.

FRANÇOIS RABELAIS

So far you've been patient. You've been waiting for me to acknowledge that there are people who are really out to get you. Some people are just plain mean and nasty, and their aim in life is to do you ill.

All right, I concede. Some people are malicious—one only needs to read the newspaper each morning to draw this conclusion. But in modern society, among the universe of difficult people, the ones who are malicious are few, and the ones who are truly evil are even fewer.

Before we assume a person is malicious, we have t
important question. Do you have a tendency to see pe
way? In other words, is there a pattern throughout yo
seeing other people as deliberately wishing you harm?

Sometimes one can erroneously interpret the actions of others as intentionally threatening or insulting. Certain personalities interpret innocent actions or remarks as having malicious intent and tend to be unforgiving when insulted or slighted.

So it is conceivable that others aren't out to get you after all; it may just look that way from your vantage point.

It is wise to begin by not assuming that someone is deliberately out to get you. When you do, it cuts off ways of improving the situation. If you think that someone wants to harm you, then you will be preoccupied with thoughts of defending yourself or getting even. You will be taken over by feelings of fear and anger. These responses are appropriate if you are truly in danger, but if you aren't, they'll just make the whole thing worse.

Avoid making the assumption that a difficult person is malicious until there is irrefutable evidence.

A Few Are Evil

Those who commit terrible deeds are not monsters. They are human beings who have done monstrous things. If they truly were beasts, they would be blameless. They are human and responsible because they have betrayed their humanness.

DAVID J. WOLPE

During the five years that I've taught workshops based on the material in this book, no topic has stirred participants as much as the subject of evil. Some demand to know whether evil really exists. Others want me to give them permission to label a difficult person in their life as evil. Still others are practical—they want to know what makes a person evil and how to face such a person when they encounter one.

It would be much easier for me to ignore the subject altogether. But I feel an obligation and a compulsion to raise these issues. First, because taking a spiritual approach toward difficult people demands that evil be considered. And second, because of my own transgenerational encounter with evil, which forces me to periodically face the demons of ancestral memory lurking in my own heart.

The horrors of the Holocaust live inside me. I cannot explain how the torturous emotions spawned by the evils my father and his family experienced were silently passed on. The science of genetics does not account for this transmission. But through some mysterious means, the sparks of feeling leapt from his heart to mine.

They linger there, quietly, until they are triggered. I could be watching the news or reading a book. They surface abruptly whenever I have a secondhand encounter with the loathsome cruelty and brutality that only evil can produce. I become overwhelmingly outraged at those who abandon their humanity to harm others. Afterward, even though the feelings pass, I continue to shudder and feel scared, more by the intensity of what is submerged within me than by the evil acts that gave rise to my reaction.

For several thousand years, theologians and philosophers of all spiritual traditions have addressed the overwhelming reality of human evil. At the core of their inquiries have been the many contradictions and paradoxes that arise when one contemplates its existence in a universe created by a God of goodness.

While I feel entirely inadequate to address these very significant questions, I am reluctantly willing to make a few statements about difficult people for the sake of this discussion. Evil exists; some difficult people, a small percentage, are evil. Evil acts can be defined. And evil can be faced and overcome under the right circumstances.

Caution is in order here. One should be very, very careful before labeling someone as evil. The term has power and terror; if we wrongly assign it to an enemy, we are giving them a dark strength they don't deserve.

A truly evil person has four distinguishing attributes.

First, an evil person engages in acts that cause harm—grievous, lingering, sorrowful harm. Evil is antithetical to life, love, and happiness.

Second, an evil person commits acts that are consciously and intentionally repeated—the evildoer knows what he or she is doing each time. Evil is a deliberate plan of action.

Third, an evildoer has a warped justification for his or her actions—in the depraved mind of the perpetrator, the victim is somehow deserving of this treatment. Evil is always targeted at someone else who is supposedly evil. An evildoer is utterly incapable of looking within at his or her own evilness and unconsciously projects it onto others and the environment.

Fourth, an evildoer has no remorse. The normal human responses of guilt and regret that operate when one hurts another are somehow lacking.

Thinking about evil is not pleasant. In fact, giving it attention only gives it sustenance. There is, however, one overriding consideration that makes it vital to discuss, and that is what to do if it is encountered.

In the previous chapter, we saw that there were many different ways of responding to a difficult person. But if someone is evil—that is, if they possess all the attributes of an evil person just described—only two responses are realistic. The first is to get away as quickly as possible and avoid future contact. The second is to resist and overcome. I usually advocate the former only because the latter demands so much more emotionally and spiritually than most of us possess.

Since evil is bent on destruction, it cannot be reasoned with, or placated, or avenged. The smartest course in most inter-personal situations is to get away. This is not cowardice, it is prudence.

Yet leaving doesn't eliminate the evil; it just eliminates its immediate effect on our well-being. There are times when evil must be resisted for the benefit of others or society as a whole. This always needs to be done through collective action, not indi-vidual valor.

Exercise great caution before labeling a difficult person as evil. But if it turns out that someone is indeed an evil person, exercise great caution in his presence and quickly remove yourself from his sphere of influence.

Giving Difficult People the Benefit of the Doubt

For nothing worthy proving can be proven,
Nor yet disproven; wherefore thou be wise,
Cleave ever to the sunnier side of doubt.

ALFRED, LORD TENNYSON

So far in this chapter we've seen that there are many possible rea-sons why someone can be difficult. A person could be clueless, stuck in the past, or preoccupied with personal struggles. He could be addicted to an ideal, a material goal, or a chemical. She could be physically or mentally ill. Or we could be the source of the difficulties by misreading the situation or using ineffective influence strategies or not acknowledging different points of view. None of these reasons would lead you to conclude that the person intentionally wishes you harm; actually, most difficult people out there are doing the best they can, given their limitations. Ineptitude is the most likely explanation for being difficult; malice and evil the least.

All this leads to a useful rule of thumb. Give difficult people the benefit of the doubt. Assume there is an interpretation for their behavior that reflects favorably on them. Consider the possibility that there is a plausible explanation for what they've done.

If you find this hard to do, reverse roles. Now *you* are the difficult person in someone else's eyes. If you were the wrongdoer, wouldn't you want others to give *you* the benefit of the doubt? Wouldn't you want them to assume you didn't mean any harm? Wouldn't you hope that people would make the assumption that there was a simple explanation for what you did?

If you are reluctant to judge a difficult person favorably, then you are basically stating that you won't give someone else the same courtesy that you would want given to you. Sort of a double standard, isn't it?

It is important to recognize that giving someone the benefit of the doubt is not tantamount to offering your approval. It does not excuse unacceptable behavior or criminal acts. It does not prevent you from taking subsequent action to recover loss or from pursuing a remedy in court. It does not keep you from protecting yourself or your property. It doesn't mean pretending that everything is fine when it isn't. It doesn't require you to just resign yourself to accepting things as they are.

What it does do is to keep you from acting rashly by drawing premature or incorrect conclusions. Giving someone the benefit of the doubt means that you are willing to consider the possibility that you don't have all the facts and might not be seeing the whole picture. It means that you are willing to extend to the other person your silent goodwill until all the evidence is in. It means that in your personal life you practice the same principle that applies in a court of law: Difficult people are innocent until proven guilty.

In an encounter with a difficult person, always assume, at least initially, that the person is trying to do the best he or she can and that there is a redeeming explanation for the difficult behavior.

The Value of Understanding Why

To understand everything is to forgive everything.

FRENCH PROVERB

Earlier in this book, we discussed how the defining characteristic of a difficult person is the fact that we experience negative emotions in reaction to that person's behavior. But our emotional response to a difficult person is not a given. It can change, depending on our perceptions.

A few years ago, while shopping, I took the risk of parking for a short while in a private lot after unsuccessfully cruising around for twenty minutes to find a space on the street. To indicate that I wouldn't be long, I left my hazard light blinking and, without realizing it, left the car unlocked. Upon returning, I was horrified to find my passenger door open and someone inside my car. I screamed at the person to get out immediately, only to see an elderly, scared man emerge. He had assumed I belonged there, noticed my hazard lights blinking, and was merely trying to prevent an eventual dead battery. My outrage turned instantly to embarrassment and appreciation.

On another occasion, a friend was driving in a downpour and spotted a fourteen-year-old girl from the neighborhood jogging down the street toward home without a coat or umbrella. He pulled up, rolled down his window, and offered her a ride. But she failed to recognize him, declined the offer, and started running as fast as she could. He suddenly realized that he must have frightened her and called her home later to assure her and her parents that she had been in no danger. Her incorrect assessment of the situation had generated great fear.

In both cases, a person's emotional response was linked to the way that person perceived a situation. In the first story, a rapid shift in my perception of the man led to an instant shift of emotion. In the second, the girl's fear gave way to relief once the truth of the situation emerged.

The way we feel is linked to the way we see. If we can change the way we see a difficult person, we can change the way we feel about them. Herein lies one pathway to relief.

Perhaps you now realize why I've devoted an entire chapter of this book to the various reasons why a person might be difficult. By taking the time to ask yourself why, and cultivating the habit of reserving judgment, you may end up revising the way you view difficult situations. And the way you feel about them may end up changing as well. By developing the practice of understanding why people are difficult, you can nurture in yourself new ways of seeing and new ways of feeling.

Asking why doesn't come easily to those who are quick to draw conclusions. If you are the type who likes to have things figured out right away, asking why will make you uncomfortable, because the process does not lead to definite answers. It leads instead to possibilities. It allows you to consider multiple explanations. It keeps you from condemning another person until you know the whole story.

Every interpersonal situation can be viewed from a variety of angles and interpreted in a variety of ways. If you've ever talked to both parties going through a divorce, you'll know exactly what I mean. We've all heard the fable of the blind men whose description of an elephant depended on what part of the elephant they were touching. When someone is being difficult, we don't know the whole story, and until we do, it is wiser not to make judgments.

In an encounter with a difficult person, it is important for us to challenge our perceptions and rethink our assumptions rather than make a quick assessment. If we judge the other person prematurely, we lock ourselves into a way of seeing and feeling that may not easily extricate us from the difficulties.

Let's consider an example. Suppose your boss has not been giving you sufficient assistance lately. Your frustration has been growing steadily, since you now have to spend additional time figuring things out on your own. Your immediate conclusion might be that he is unhappy with your work, or that he is a lousy manager, or that you are about to be laid off. These perceptions can only lead to feelings of fear or anger.

But what if it turns out that you were wrong? What if your boss has just been reprimanded by *his* boss and is worried about his own job? What if he has just received an offer from another company and has already left the job mentally? What if he is a recovering alcoholic who recently started drinking again? Or what if you were to learn that he is preoccupied because his sixteen-year-old son has just been in an auto accident? With each different explanation, your feelings will change. For the last possibility mentioned, your anger at his inattentiveness might quickly turn into compassion for his family tragedy.

Consider another example. Suppose your elderly neighbor is constantly accusing you of spying on her. Maybe she is being spied on, but by someone else. Maybe she is having paranoid delusions and needs psychiatric help. Maybe her accusations are a side effect of a powerful drug she is taking for an acute medical condition. Considering these possibilities may lead you to feel sympathy for her plight rather than feeling attacked.

When dealing with a difficult person, cultivate the habit of asking yourself why the person might be difficult. It will help you start the process of healing.

Suffering, Deprivation, Ignorance, and Compassion

If we could read the secret history of our enemies, we should find in each person's life sorrow and suffering enough to disarm all hostility.

HENRY WADSWORTH LONGFELLOW

If we look back at the various explanations for difficult behavior in this chapter, we find common threads. Almost all difficult behaviors result from suffering, deprivation, or ignorance. People do the things they do to other people because they hurt, they want, or they don't know.

We may despise those who cause us harm. We may condemn their acts. But we cannot, with absolute certainty, maintain that we would not do the same if we had lived through the same troubles and afflictions.

When I was growing up, some of the things my father said to me and to my brothers hurt us. But I always knew, even as a young boy, that he had endured experiences in Nazi slave labor camps that I would never, ever begin to comprehend. Later in life, I came around to forgiving him. I knew the behaviors that hurt me so much originated in his own unhealed anguish. I knew he was basically a kind person who didn't realize the impact he had on his children and was doing the best he could with the horrible memories he carried.

Ultimately, any sincere effort to understand why others are difficult must lead one to feel compassion for the suffering, deprivation, and ignorance at the root of all difficult behavior.

Separating the Person from the Difficulties

Let a man always consider himself as if the Holy One dwells within him.

THE TALMUD

No matter what a difficult person might do, that person is a fellow human being first; the difficult aspect is secondary. As much as we might not want to admit it, each person has just as much of a right to be here as we do.

The part of difficult people that we find difficult is not their true nature, it is not who they really are. Difficult behaviors are often just misguided and unconscious ways of dealing with life's challenges, hurts, and travails. Difficult people want the same attention, respect, and love that we all do—they just try to get it in ways that create problems for others.

If we choose to relate to difficult people by focusing only on the behaviors that bother us so much, then without realizing it we are contributing to keeping them stuck where they are. We are reinforcing the self-image and set of erroneous beliefs about reality that perpetuate the difficult behaviors.

We are all spiritual beings. The differences between us merely reflect the degree to which we realize this. For difficult people, the inner light is obscured, but it is not absent. Goodness and holiness do reside within each of us.

So the secret of relating to a difficult person is to relate to the whole person. Silently recognize and acknowledge that the person is also created in the image of God. Appreciate the goodness that is hidden deeply behind the difficult behavior.

By looking for the good in others, we bring out the best instead of the beast.

Explorations

UNDERSTANDING WHY

Purpose: To develop the habit of asking yourself why someone might be difficult

Choose a difficult person in your life. Now make a list of all the reasons you can think of that might explain that person's behavior. Use the categories in this chapter as a starting point, adding your own.

Begin with the obvious reasons, and don't finish your list until you have also come up with reasons that are implausible and even far-fetched. For example, if your boss is always yelling at you, the most obvious reasons might be that he is under constant stress from his boss or that he grew up in a home where yelling was the normal way of communicating. The most far-fetched reasons might be that he is rehearsing for a part in a play or has been replaced by an evil alien creature. These two might seem silly to you, but as you answer the questions below, you'll see why it is just as useful to list them as it is to list the plausible reasons.

Once you have completed your own list, share your situation with a friend or two and see if they can come up with additional reasons that didn't occur to you.

Now review your list and reflect on each of the following questions:

- How much do you really know about the difficult person's life and background? Is your assessment based on concrete information or on assumptions and conjecture?
- What specific additional information would you need to acquire from the person or from other sources to really understand why she acts the way she does?

- How many different plausible reasons exist for explaining the behavior?
- How many additional reasons did your friends add to your list that didn't occur to you?
- How accurate do you think your perception of the situation is?
- If you were to describe the situation to someone who is not connected with you or the difficult person, would that person perceive the situation the same way you do?
- Have you been giving the person the benefit of the doubt or assuming negative intent and malice?
- How have your emotional reactions to the situation shifted as you consider various alternative explanations?
- When you consider some of the more far-fetched explanations, does it help you laugh about your situation and lighten your heart?
- Given what you know about the other person, how would you behave if you were in that person's shoes? Would you also engage in the same difficult behaviors?

CHAPTER 4

THE HAND OF THE HOLY ONE

Viewing Difficult Relationships from a Spiritual Perspective

It is human misery and not pleasure which contains the secret of divine wisdom.

SIMONE WEIL

In chapter 3, we considered how our feelings about a difficult person could change once we acquired a deeper understanding of the reasons the person was being difficult. To review a basic principle, the way we feel about something depends upon the way in which we see it.

This chapter will provide yet another way of "seeing" our difficult relationships. This time we'll view the difficult people in our lives as teachers. By taking a spiritual perspective, we'll examine our difficulties not as chance occurrences but as events that have a purpose. Instead of seeing each difficult person as a nemesis, we will look at him or her as someone who has been sent to us with the potential to help us on our spiritual journey.

The most difficult people have the potential to become our very best teachers, because the adversity that we experience in a difficult relationship can help us to overcome resistance and teach us what we would fail to otherwise learn.

At the start of this book, I pointed out that the Bible is filled with stories about difficult people. Since one of the purposes of the Bible is to teach about God and God's relationship with humanity, it is indeed fascinating that the author(s) deliberately chose to present these teachings in the context of stories about difficult relationships.

There is a spiritual meaning in our interpersonal struggles.

Anyone Can Be a Teacher

Who is a wise person? One who learns from everyone.

BEN ZOMA *(Pirke Avot 4:1)*

At one point in my thirties I was an obnoxious intellectual snob. Unfortunately I still carry remnants of those days. My snobbery was instilled during graduate school, when I was taught that only certain scholars, certain scholarly journals, certain research methods, and certain universities were worthwhile. Anything written by an unknown scholar affiliated with a second-rate school that appeared in an inferior journal using substandard research methods was beneath contempt. And even worse was anything written by anyone who didn't have the proper academic credentials.

It may be hard for you to believe that people actually think this way, but I've met lots of them. They tend to inhabit the best colleges and universities.

My snobbery started to erode once I started teaching and realized that my students had just as much to teach me as I had to teach them. It was a different kind of learning than I was used to, based on life, not books. My students taught me about aspiration and disappointment, about fairness and discovery and respect and caring. They taught me how to use the power I possessed in the classroom responsibly, how to communicate in a way that touched and inspired them, what made them laugh with me, and what made them lose respect for me.

Gradually I started to realize that I could learn from everyone I encountered. I could learn just as much from a panhandler as from a Ph.D. if I was open to the possibility.

Everyone has something to teach us. What we can learn might or might not be obvious, and it might or might not be something we're interested in learning. But from our side, if we are attentive and receptive, we will be surprised at the information and insight that other people offer just by being who they are.

Let me share an illustrative story. In the midst of my writing this book, the transmission of my faithful nine-year-old car began to break down. With the car's odometer reading of 162,000 miles, I wanted to drop big money on a repair about as much as I wanted a hernia operation. But the alternative, getting another car and taking on new car payments, would have cost even more at a time when money was tight. So I located a reputable repair shop and lumbered there in second gear.

The owner got behind the wheel, and the two of us went for a ride to diagnose the problem. In between comical lurches, he asked me what I did, and I told him I was writing a book about how to deal with difficult people. Excited, he began to tell me his own tale about dealing with difficult customers. Our drive lengthened.

Transmission shops deal with difficult people every day, because no one wants to be there. No one willingly pays up to $1,500 with a smile just to get their car back after several days so it once again does what it's supposed to do in the first place. Even though it's a tough way to make a living, the owner seemed to enjoy what he did and had a good relationship with his customers.

Then he explained why. When he was first married, his bank called him to tell him that his wife had bounced a check. Furious, he rushed over to tell the banker off, convinced it was the bank's mistake. In spite of his rudeness, the banker dealt with him in a calm and respectful manner, completely defusing his anger. He never forgot the way he was treated; the banker taught him a valuable method for handling irate customers that he has used ever since. He was able to learn by observing one of the banker's interpersonal strengths.

Learning from others requires humility. Whenever a friend of mine attends a public talk on a topic of interest to her, she predictably comes back to tell me all the things the speaker did wrong and all the ways in which she could have done a better job. If you already think you're smarter than someone else, then obviously you have nothing to learn from them. If you invest your mental energy in comparisons or feelings of envy, you leave no room in your mind to discover what other people can offer you.

Each person does at least one thing well, and each person does at least one thing poorly. We can learn from both. We can learn from someone who is efficient how to better organize our time. We can learn from someone who remembers our name how good it feels to be acknowledged, and how we might strive to do the same in our daily interactions. We can learn from someone who is a bad liar how obvious our own lies must be to others; we can also learn, if we're so inclined, how to be a better liar. We can learn from someone who treats us badly how unpleasant it must be for others to be at the receiving end of our own nastiness.

Anyone and everyone can be our teacher if we are receptive and acknowledge that there is always something to be learned.

The Exquisite Mystery of Relationships

Be attentive in all that you do;
do not judge one deed small and another great,
for you cannot always know their significance.

JUDAH HA NASSI *(Pirke Avot 2:1)*

Sophie Freud, a granddaughter of Sigmund Freud and retired professor of social work at a Boston area college, spoke at a conference I attended several years ago and told a poignant story. One evening, Dr. Freud related, a woman approached her after a speech she just had given. The woman, it turned out, was a former student of Dr. Freud's who had received a master's degree from the college about ten years earlier. The woman recounted how Dr. Freud had advised her at the end of her graduate studies that she was not likely to make a good social worker and should consider another profession. Dr. Freud had no recollection of the earlier conversation and was dismayed to have been so callous and discouraging.

Receiving such disheartening feedback from a prominent figure would have been crushing to some. But the woman went on to say she had come to see Dr. Freud that evening specifically to tell her that in spite of the dismaying assessment she received after so much hard work, she had resolved to excel. In fact, she had become quite successful at her profession so she could prove the advice was wrong.

The story illustrates two important aspects of relationships: first, that it is impossible to predict how our words and actions will affect others; and second, that a single interaction between two people can have repercussions for years.

In the unpredictable realm of human interaction, things just don't always seem to turn out the way we want them to. For example, our intentions may be honorable, and we may act in ways that we think are appropriate and justified, but the result may be a disaster. We can all remember times in our own lives when we thought we were doing the right thing but things didn't turn out the way we hoped. Just consider how much of history comprises stories of people with seemingly laudable goals who end up ignobly.

In contrast, we may say or do something that is ill-advised and inappropriate and find to our surprise that things turn out okay. Dr. Freud and her student are a case in point.

In recognizing that the course of our actions is ultimately unfathomable, we face a particular danger. The fact that we can't predict what will happen as a consequence of our words and actions might lead to irresponsibility. But because we are accountable for what we do, we still must act with sensitivity.

Even though we are unable to peer into the future to see the implications of our actions, we can still get a glimpse of something else—the exquisite mystery of relationships.

At every moment, in every interaction, however brief, there is potential for us to affect others. This potential can come from the most casual comments or gestures as well as the most purposeful acts.

Other people have the potential to affect our life profoundly through their actions without ever realizing it. We possess the same power.

Life Is a School and Difficult People Are the Faculty

The prudent person makes a mirror out of the evil eye of others, and it is more truthful than that of affection, and helps reduce one's defects or amend them.

BALTHAZAR GRACIÁN

So far in this chapter we've seen that everyone has the potential to be our teacher and that difficult people can teach us things about ourselves that we wouldn't otherwise learn. We've pondered how a simple interaction between two people can have an unanticipated and lasting impact.

What if these people and encounters didn't just come into our life randomly? What if they were somehow placed in our path to teach us?

Let's explore a spiritual framework for understanding our relationship difficulties based on the premise that life is like a school.

I've spent so much time in a classroom, both as a student and as a teacher, that when I first encountered the concept of life being like a school, it resonated instantly. Over the years, as my spiritual understanding has continued to broaden, this simple metaphor still lies at the core of my beliefs. The notion that we are here to learn continues to give the events of my life a much richer meaning.

Philosophers, poets, and theologians have pondered the meaning of life for so long that the very expression has become a cliché. Various religions claim to have the answer, many people assume we'll never know the answer, and there are others who argue that there are no answers.

What follows is a personal spiritual philosophy that is informed by my study of religious and spiritual traditions. It represents the tentative answers I've arrived at after years of trying to make sense of this unpredictable and mysterious life we live. I shy away from any definitive statements about the mysteries of existence because the mysteries are so utterly impenetrable and my understanding of them is still so elementary.

Let's start by examining what it means to compare life to a school. A school is a place to learn certain lessons, presented in a certain order. If you demonstrate that you have learned a particular lesson after passing certain tests, you move on to the next level of learning. If you don't pass, you just keep repeating the lesson until you do. The learning is presented by teachers, and there are also opportunities to learn on your own.

The very best schools have individually tailored lesson plans for each student. Students progress at their own speed, struggling with some lessons while mastering others quickly. The best schools have individual tutoring; each student gets the amount of attention he or she needs from the teacher best suited for the material.

So if we say that life is like a school, what kind of school are we talking about? Not just any school. The school of life is different for each person. It is difficult and painful. It is mysterious. It is remarkable and extraordinary and joyous. It is all these things and unfathomably more, because life is the school that was created for us by the Holy One.

Each of our souls is imbued with a unique and divine purpose. To fulfill that purpose, each soul must master various spiritual lessons as preparation. Life is a process of continuous learning until the soul's divine purpose is ready to be expressed in its full and magnificent splendor.

Just what are these spiritual lessons? They differ for each person. However, some lessons are so universal that we all are presented with circumstances that challenge us to master them. For example, we might be provided with specific opportunities to cultivate and express kindness, generosity, caring, or faith.

All of us have a complicated mix of character strengths and weaknesses, just as in school we might have been good at languages but weak at math. Consider, for example, someone who appears generous and gives large sums to charity but does so primarily to receive community acclaim rather than to help others. Another individual might treat family members with warmth and kindness but go to work each day and cheat customers at their business.

Just as a good school teaches something new each day, life presents us with daily opportunities to refine our character through interactions with other people. The school of life is always offering us ways to develop our spiritual qualities that remain undeveloped; the situations and events we encounter are like taking different courses.

Let's consider some examples. A self-centered person who thinks only about his own needs might be presented with an opportunity to learn how to put another first by having to care for someone with a serious illness. One who, in contrast, is selfless and thinks only about the needs of others might need to learn how to receive the same loving care by being hospitalized. A person who considers herself superior to others because of a prominent job and large income might need to experience a career setback and financial hardship to learn humility. A person with unexpressed talent might need to endure a boring job until he gets so frustrated that he finally develops the courage to leave and do what he does best.

Most of our spiritual lessons are not easy, obvious, or comfortable. The hardest ones are the ones least likely to be learned voluntarily.

Someone who is arrogant doesn't generally look to become humble. A person who is indifferent toward the needs of others doesn't suddenly seek to become caring. People who lash out in anger don't go looking to acquire self-control. People who lack generosity rarely have a change of heart and begin donating large sums to a local charity.

Because spiritual growth demands that we overcome our character flaws, and because it is so challenging to do so, we need a special teacher.

The teacher would have to be someone who would shatter our incorrect beliefs, frozen feelings, and self-delusion. Someone who would help us to break free of our current, limited understandings. Someone who could uproot the very things in life that we are most invested in holding on to and keeping the same. Someone who causes us so much pain that we finally out of desperation must begin to make the necessary changes that we have resisted for so long.

It would have to be a difficult person.

In the school of life, difficult people are the faculty. They teach us our most important spiritual lessons, the lessons that we would be most unlikely to learn on our own.

A Glimpse Behind the Scenes

Heaven at present is out of sight, but in due time, as snow melts and discovers what it lay upon, so will this visible creation fade away before those greater splendors which are behind it.

JOHN HENRY NEWMAN

We've talked about how life is like a school. Let's consider another model. Suppose life was like a movie.

When we go to a movie, unless we have studied filmmaking, we have very little idea of what actually went on behind the scenes. We enjoy the movie as entertainment without paying too much attention to its technical elements. We rarely think about the fact that almost every word of dialogue is scripted. Or that every shot has been carefully composed, every prop precisely designed, and every item of clothing meticulously chosen and tailored. We don't realize how artfully the lighting and the sound are masterminded. We don't stop to ponder how every single moment of the movie has been crafted and approved by the director, who has spent many months making the movie and then painstakingly edited every single frame.

How is life like a movie? Because life's events may appear random, but if we look behind the scenes, they aren't. God directs the universe using an infinitely complex script, astronomically magnificent sets, and billions upon billions of actors. We are part of a vast panorama without an inkling of the indescribable, hidden majesty that gives rise to all that happens on this earth.

Based on our personal experience, we may have no reason to believe that a heavenly realm exists. We have to rely on the testimony of those religious teachers, mystics, and ordinary people who have had glimpses of the holy and have shared their visions with us in their writings and teachings. There are people who have been witnesses to the divine realm. They have had a privileged look behind the scenes and have caught a glimpse of the Director.

Understandably, many refuse to accept such personal testimony and deny that there is anything more to life than what our senses can perceive. Perhaps another analogy will help to illustrate why such a worldview can be limited.

In the past few years, cellular phones have become commonplace. They work because of an elaborate, sophisticated, and largely invisible network of hardware and software that took years to develop. Living everyday life while denying the existence of a higher reality is similar to using a cellular phone while denying the existence of the infrastructure that makes its use possible. Just because one doesn't see the network when using the phone doesn't mean there isn't one.

Of course, cellular phone networks are tangible; one can verify that the network exists by touring the facilities. There isn't yet a comparable tour of the realm of the holy. Meditation, prayer, study, and faith do eventually provide us with access; the amount of time it takes is different for each person and is proportionate to effort and sincere desire.

The "infrastructure" of heaven is indescribably complex. For our purposes, however, there is one simple point about it that has relevance. The unseen spiritual domain is completely capable of placing specific people in our path to help us learn a specific lesson.

So difficult people don't just come into our lives randomly. We are drawn to them, or they are drawn to us, to help us learn our spiritual lessons. They appear in our lives because they have certain qualities that can help us on our spiritual journey. Difficult people have just what we need to help us overcome our character flaws.

We should always remind ourselves that difficulties in our relationships may not be chance occurrences. Difficult people could be in our life for a reason.

Tests

Search me, O God, and know my heart;
test me and know my thoughts.
And see if I have vexing ways;
and lead me in the way of eternity.

PSALM 139:23–24

The hardest part of going to school is tests. I say that as someone who has taken, written, and graded many thousands of tests over the years. No one likes taking tests but they continue to be used because in most cases they are the best way to determine if something has been learned.

The situations we face in our dealings with difficult people are often sent to us as tests. We are tested to see if we have mastered certain lessons—for example, restraining our fury, resisting the desire for revenge, or standing up for ourselves when we are being mistreated.

The idea that God sends tests is ancient. For example, chapter

22 of Genesis describes Abraham's experience when God asks him to sacrifice his son Isaac, perhaps the most demanding spiritual test one could ever face.

Fortunately, the tests we encounter most of the time aren't as stark. Usually they are presented to us as choices. They could involve a choice between doing what's easy or doing what's right. They might require us to choose between forgiveness and vengeance, or between tolerance and condemnation. A test might require us to take decisive action when our usual inclination is to pretend that everything is fine even though it isn't. Or to remain patient when our usual inclination is to act impulsively.

Tests are repeated if we fail them. If we continue to ignore the spiritual lessons being presented, they get harder.

Once I spent the night at a hotel in Zurich. The hotel room had a type of alarm clock built into the headboard that I'd never seen before. I figured out how it worked, set it to my wake-up time, and went to sleep.

The next morning, while I was lying half awake, it chimed about fifteen minutes before it was set to go off. Faintly, almost imperceptibly, I heard four very gentle ascending tones. Five minutes later, the clock chimed again with the same pattern, but a bit more audibly this time. And after another five minutes, it chimed even louder. By wake-up time, the chime was at full volume, but by now I was fully awake.

In my workshops, I often compare this Swiss alarm to the way in which the Universe operates—both try to wake us up in a way that progressively gets our attention. Divine hints start out gently; if we are awake already, we can pass our tests easily. But if we don't pay attention, and we remain asleep, then the tests start getting harder and harder, and the signals get louder and louder.

Have you ever noticed how the same types of difficulties tend to be found under different circumstances? How you might leave a job to get away from a demanding boss only to end up with a boss who is even more demanding? How you may end a relationship with a partner who is critical only to chose another one who is even more faultfinding? How you might move to get away from a noisy and inconsiderate neighbor only to end up with a construction crew next door to your new home?

Tests are presented to us in various forms until we learn what we're supposed to be learning. That is why leaving as an option for dealing with difficult people isn't necessarily effective. Our difficulties keep following us until we have learned the spiritual lesson that is being presented. Remember, what happens to us isn't random.

Most of the time, the tests we are given in life are not easily recognized. If our spiritual tests and the lessons we were supposed to be learning were obvious, then passing the test would only prove that we knew how to do what we were supposed to do. It wouldn't show spiritual learning and character development, just our willingness to obey and follow the rules. If we knew about our tests in advance, the element of choice would be taken away. We need to make our spiritual choices through our own free will, not because we are fearful of the consequences of breaking the rules.

While we are being tested, life can be terribly painful, and the meaning of our challenge is usually elusive. It may seem like the height of insensitivity for someone to tell us that our difficulties and suffering are for our spiritual betterment.

But once we have successfully passed a spiritual test and mastered the lesson it presents, we receive the blessing of insight. We are able to look back and see what it was that we needed to learn, as well as the reasons why we needed to learn it. We come to understand the role of the difficult people in our life and why a particular person was sent to teach us. It might take days or a lifetime, but eventually, we do get an answer to the "why" question that has been weighing down our heart for so long.

In a situation with a difficult person, it is always helpful to ask yourself: If this is happening for a reason, then what am I supposed to be learning?

Difficult People Teach Us How Our Actions Affect Others

African Religion: One going to take a pointed stick to pinch a baby bird should first try it on himself to feel how it hurts.

NIGERIAN PROVERB

Buddhism: Just as I am so are they; just as they are so am I.

SUTTA NIPATA

Christianity: Whatever you wish that men would do to you, do so to them.

MATTHEW 7:12

Confucianism: Do not do to others what you do not want them to do to you.

ANALECTS OF CONFUCIUS

Hinduism: One should not behave toward others in a way which is disagreeable to oneself.

MAHABHARATA

Islam: Not one of you is a believer until he loves for his brother what he loves for himself.

FORTY HADITH OF AN-NAWAWI

Judaism: Love your fellow as yourself.

LEVITICUS 19:18

The Golden Rule is the most fundamental spiritual lesson. It is the one spiritual teaching that everyone knows, yet most of us don't practice it consciously or conscientiously on a daily basis.

The Talmud contains a story about a nonbeliever who approaches a teacher named Shammai and asks to be taught Torah while he stands on one foot. Shammai is so incensed at the insolence of this man that he strikes the nonbeliever with his rod. The nonbeliever approaches Hillel and makes the same request. But this time he receives a response: *What is hateful to you, do not do to your neighbor—that is the whole Torah; all the rest is commentary. Go and learn.*

How then do we learn what is hateful? One way is through our interactions with difficult people.

Difficult people teach us what it is like to be at the receiving end of thoughtless, uncaring, insensitive behavior. Difficult people show us how unpleasant it is to be treated badly. Difficult people remind us to treat others with honor and respect because they provide us with an unmatched opportunity to learn about what is hateful.

There is yet another way of viewing difficult people in relation to the Golden Rule. Chapter 1, verse 26 of Genesis reads, *God said: Let us make man in our image, after our likeness.* If we are indeed made in the image of God, then to treat another person with disrespect is to desecrate a holy image. That is the core truth of the Golden Rule.

Every difficult person who comes into our lives is a reminder to us to follow the Golden Rule.

Difficult People Do unto Us as We Have Done unto Others

I the Lord probe the heart,
Search the mind—
To repay every man according to his ways,
With the proper fruit of his deeds.

JEREMIAH 17:10

Gina and Mike dated for several years and, like many couples, had lots of fun when they weren't fighting. But whenever Mike did something that upset Gina, regardless of what it was, she responded with nasty comments about his weight. Mike had always been chubby and was particularly sensitive to such remarks; Gina knew that and used his vulnerability to get him back for the hurt he supposedly caused her.

After a while, Mike finally got wise and began to make it clear that her tactics constituted dirty fighting—if she had a problem with something he did, she had the right to express her feelings but did not have the right to attack him in a deliberately hurtful way about something unrelated to her complaint. Gina ignored his requests and continued to berate him about his girth.

As you might have guessed, the relationship came to an end, and Gina subsequently married Randy, who did not have issues with food. Ironically, after the marriage, Gina put on some pounds herself, but Randy didn't mind, and their marriage was a happy one.

One day Gina's college roommate arrived for a visit. Laura, a fitness trainer, lived in another city and hadn't seen Gina since the wedding; she noticed Gina's weight gain immediately but didn't comment on it, at least not right away.

At the end of a shopping trip the next day, the two old friends got out of a subway train, Gina first. Laura, unable to hold her tongue any longer, said, "You should see what you look like from behind!" Gina was utterly devastated by her friend's unkind remark, and the sting remained for several weeks.

After time passed and the hurt subsided, Gina started to realize how uncanny it was that Laura's remark resembled the barbed criticisms she used to make about Mike. Now she knew how it must have felt to him. She ended up resolving to avoid making nasty comments in the future, turning the experience into a learning opportunity.

As discussed earlier, the Golden Rule tells us to do unto others as we would have them do unto us. But many don't realize that there is a footnote to the Golden Rule in fine print, which reads: *Caution! If you ignore this rule, someone will eventually come along and do unto you as you have done unto others!*

> **Another way that we can view a difficult person is as a cosmic courier, unwittingly delivering the fruits of our deeds. Difficult people enable us to experience the same hurt we have inflicted on another.**

Is There Divine Justice?

> *If God's justice could be recognized as just by human comprehension, it would not be divine.*
>
> MARTIN LUTHER

All spiritual traditions teach the message that the universe is governed by justice. As the popular saying goes, what goes around, comes around.

In the East, the concept is called *karma*, a term that simply means action. Each action, according to this outlook, has consequences flowing from its merit; positive action brings positive effects to the doer, negative actions bring negative effects.

Unfortunately, the idea of karma tends to be dismissed in the West, associated a little too closely with the psychedelic era of the late 1960s and the hippie phrase, "bad karma." Yet the concept itself, minus its Eastern label, is very much a part of Western spiritual thought.

For example, in Genesis we find the notion of divine justice in the well-known story of Jacob. Chapter 27 describes how Jacob, with the assistance of his mother Rebecca, fools his father Isaac into bestowing upon him the blessing of the firstborn, stealing it from his older brother Esau, the rightful recipient. Yet a little later, Jacob himself is fooled in similar fashion by his mother's wily brother Laban.

Chapter 29 of Genesis describes how Jacob falls in love with Laban's daughter Rachel and offers to work seven years to wed her. At the end of that time, a wedding does occur, but Laban deceives Jacob at the last second by substituting his older daughter Leah for the younger Rachel.

The correspondences are striking. Jacob deceives his father to get what he wants; he is in turn deceived by Laban, who prevents Jacob from getting what he wants. Jacob substitutes himself, the younger brother, for the older; Laban substitutes the older sister for the younger. Jacob's guile is instigated by his mother, Rebecca; Laban, the perpetrator of Jacob's undoing, is Rebecca's brother.

In the New Testament as well we find mention of divine justice. For example, in Galatians 6:7: "whatever a man sows, that he will also reap." In Matthew 16:27: "For the Son of Man is to come with his angels in the glory of his Father, and then he will repay every man for what he has done." And Matthew 26:52: "All who take the sword will perish by the sword."

A literal reading of the Bible and a superficial understanding of karma would lead one to believe that divine justice is dispensed as a fearsome punishment, meted out to those who have acted wickedly. If we take a strict religious viewpoint, we would be advised to treat others well to avoid God's wrath. Punishments for transgressions against one's fellow man or woman are inexorable. Fortunately, divine justice is not simply punitive, or fear would be our only motivation for being nice to people.

The term *punishment*, used so often in religion, is both misleading and harsh. Divine justice is not merely punishment—it is retribution tempered by kindness and mercy. Divine justice comes to us only when we are ready for it—when it can serve the purpose of advancing our spiritual growth, ultimately helping us on our spiritual journey as we learn to become more sensitive, caring, and loving toward others. We reap what we have sown in order to learn, not merely to suffer.

So divine justice is not necessarily dispensed measure for measure. It comes back to us in a manner that is best suited for teaching us what we need to learn. This should provide some peace of mind to those who have committed wrongs in the past. One does not need to be apprehensive about divine justice if one experiences life's events in a spiritual fashion and is sincere about becoming a better person. If one genuinely strives to grow and feels remorse for the errors one has committed in the past, the Universe will be gentle rather than severe. Karma cannot be expunged, but it can be softened through charitable acts, prayer, and sincere repentance.

This is why malicious revenge, discussed in chapter 2, is so ill-advised. By consciously and deliberately choosing to harm another, we are sowing the seeds of future karmic retribution. And since our motives have not been noble, divine justice will not be gentle.

In light of this discussion, it is reasonable to ask about those who seem to get away with outrageous antisocial behavior that harms others. Where then is the justice for those who act destructively?

Woody Allen addressed this quandary as the central theme in his movie *Crimes and Misdemeanors*. One character literally gets away with murder while another, whose life is devoted to doing good, goes blind. At the end of the movie, the viewer is left feeling that life is terribly unjust.

While Woody Allen might make entertaining films, his theological views differ considerably from the religious mainstream. Spiritual traditions are consistent in teaching that one always reaps what one sows; what differs from one tradition to another is the timing and the way that one receives divine justice.

Christianity, for example, describes consequences in the afterlife. Jewish mystical teachings, Buddhism, and Hinduism all uphold a belief in reincarnation, maintaining that if one does not experience the consequences of one's actions in this life, one will experience them in future lives.

It is not within the scope of this book to debate the merits of each religious position. But it is important to recognize that, while one's actions toward others may not necessarily result in immediate consequences, all spiritual traditions teach that our behavior is ultimately rewarded or punished. To deny the concept of justice altogether is to accept the premise that the Universe is random and one can act with impunity unless one manages to get caught.

Hence the apparent perception that evil acts go unpunished. From a cosmic perspective, there is no point in punishing someone immediately and harshly when it would merely cause that person to become even more embittered and destructive. Society's mechanism for punishing wrongdoing when the wrongdoer is apprehended protects the public from further criminal acts but generally fails to rehabilitate. Jails are filled with hardened, unrepentant criminals who would continue to commit crimes if they were able. Human justice and divine justice have separate but intersecting aims.

As we've discussed, cosmic justice is never solely punitive. It is intended to help us see the error of our ways so that we strive toward a more lofty standard of behavior.

However, there is a catch. We are only given opportunities for growth and change, not assurances. It is up to us to recognize and interpret the events that the Universe sends us, understanding what may seem on the surface to be something negative in its true divine light. When something bad happens to us, it actually means there is potential for us to learn from it, or it wouldn't have happened at that time.

Some people grow up in terrible environments and overcome them to become remarkable achievers. Others don't. We are not powerless victims of life's experiences—we always have a choice about how we respond and what we become. The loving Universe that we inhabit is ever hopeful that we choose the path of spiritual uplift. When we don't, we are always given new opportunities.

Applying all this to the difficult people in our lives leads us to the conclusion that difficult people must be serving as emissaries of divine justice. Difficult people teach us what we have done to others in the past, giving us reason and inspiration to act differently in the future.

Reflecting for a moment, we come to realize that behind the scenes a magnificent sense of humor is operating. Think of it—the wondrous workings of divine justice, dispensed in an infinitely complex but ultimately loving fashion for each soul, routed through . . . your mother-in-law. Just how divine justice ends up getting dispatched through the behaviors of our boss, neighbor, or dry cleaner is certainly a mystery—but then, the Universe works in ways that are both mysterious and humorous.

> **The next time someone treats you badly, ask yourself if you've ever done something similar to someone else in the past, and if you have, resolve with all sincerity not to do it again.**

Difficult People Teach Us What Not to Do

*When you see a good man think of emulating him; when
you see a bad man, examine your own heart.*

CONFUCIUS

So far, we have presented the concept of divine justice as one possible explanation for the difficult people in our life. The Universe
may have placed difficult people in our path so that we can experience the same hurt that we have previously inflicted on another.
The purpose—to inspire a change of heart.

If we take this spiritual logic a step further, we can conceive of
another explanation for the presence of difficult people. Perhaps
difficult people are in our path not because we have hurt another
in the past, but so that we don't hurt someone in the future. In
other words, a difficult person can serve as a sort of early preven-
tion system, someone whose awfulness motivates us to resolve,
"I'll never do that!" Difficult people teach us what *not* to do.

Stan, as one example, was scared sober by his father and older
brother, who were both alcoholics. Stan grew up experiencing all
the worst qualities of not one but two drunks. As he grew up, he
decided never to drink and never to subject anyone to what he had
had to endure.

Much of my own philosophy as a teacher came not from a
mentor but from what I hated as a student. Right at the start of my
career, I resolved that I would not engage in the sorts of teaching
practices that I had found so distasteful in my own schooling. I did
the opposite of what had been done to me.

Unfortunately, not everyone learns positive things from negative experiences. Some people who are mistreated immediately
turn around and mistreat someone else at the first opportunity.
This can happen for two reasons.

Some people harm others mindlessly, as an unconscious way to injure the one who injured them. These people are unable to make the connection between the pain they experience and the pain they cause to innocent parties.

For others, doing to someone else what has been done to them is a deliberate and calculated act, a way, however distorted and ineffective, to understand the mind of the original perpetrator.

These patterns are all too common in families, where the mistakes of one generation are passed down and perpetuated by the next. Those who have been abused become abusers. The spiritual imperative for anyone in these circumstances is to break the chain.

Difficult people serve as reverse role models. They teach us how not to treat others.

Difficult People Teach Us to Be Cautious

Mishaps are like knives, that either serve us or cut us, as we grasp them by the blade or the handle.

JAMES RUSSELL LOWELL

Kurt was recruited into a cult while he was in college. During a time when he was lonely and life seemed meaningless, he was approached by a pair of friendly women around his age in the student union. They showed interest in him and listened to him and then invited him to a free weekend retreat where he would meet nice people and learn some fascinating things. He decided to go, and while some of the ideas seemed strange and difficult to understand, he was welcomed by the group with a love that he had never experienced. He soon joined and dropped out of school. The group seemed to embody what he'd always been looking for.

Kurt remained in the cult for eleven years. He was taught to adore the cult leader, who was said to possess a special relation-

ship with God. The leader's every word was videotaped for pos-
terity, and his writings were published in elaborately printed vol-
umes. The leader would sit on a lavishly decorated stage and speak
in a rambling fashion for hours without a break about the most
abstract ideas. At the end of these sessions Kurt had no idea what
the leader had been talking about, but he assumed it had to be
profound and that his inability to understand reflected his own
limited spiritual development.

Slowly, over the course of several years, Kurt began to question the leader's lifestyle and way of running the organization. The
leader's relatives all seemed to be affluent and hold positions of
power. Followers worked long hours without pay, and if they had
health problems, they were asked to leave instead of receiving
care. Anyone who questioned the leader's teachings was considered a troublemaker and had privileges taken away; if the questions continued, the person would be asked to leave as well.

Kurt's doubts continued to grow. A friend from his college
days recommended that Kurt read a recently published book
about cults. The book confirmed his observations and was just
what he needed to give him the motivation to finally leave.

Several years of disorientation followed as Kurt tried to estab-
lish a new identity and life outside the cult. He went to postcult
support groups and saw a therapist, the author of the book he'd
read, whose specialty was working with people who had been in
cults.

Kurt learned many things about himself and about the mind-
control techniques that cults use to recruit followers. He acquired
a new appreciation of how deceit and manipulation are used to
influence people throughout society. Eventually he returned to
graduate school so that he could earn a counseling degree to help
other cult victims.

The world is not always a safe place. Some people overreact
and respond to life by being paranoid and distrustful. Others are

too trusting and naive. People can be fooled and tricked by cults, scam artists, fraudulent investment schemes, dishonest businesses, and other individuals and groups that prey on those who are gullible. Sometimes the only way to learn to be vigilant is to be cheated or deceived.

> **Difficult people teach us to be careful in our dealings with others. The Universe may send a deceitful person into our life so that we learn caution and are protected from even greater harm in the future.**

Difficult People Give Us an Opportunity to Teach Others

A good example is the best sermon.

THOMAS FULLER

We've pointed out that in dealing with a difficult person, we always have choices. We can choose to hold a grudge, or we can let go of it. We can be embittered, or we can forgive. We can respond to nasty behavior with nastiness of our own, or we can exercise restraint. We can plot to get even, or we can resist the temptation to do so.

Our choices have implications. Inappropriate choices further alienate the person with whom we're having difficulties. If we attempt to do harm in a spirit of vindictiveness, our choices sow the seeds for future karmic retribution. In contrast, appropriate choices help both sides to move toward reconciliation and healing.

But our choices don't just affect us, and they don't just affect the difficult person with whom we're dealing. Each time we make a choice, others may be watching. They could be our children, our coworkers, or those just passing by. Each person who is a witness can't help but observe our behavior, react to it, and learn from it.

So a key issue when we are dealing with a difficult person has to do with the kind of example that we are setting.

There could be times when we encounter difficult people so that we can model appropriate behavior for others. The purpose of the difficulties might be so that others have an opportunity to observe and learn from the way that we respond.

History gives us examples of people like Mahatma Gandhi or Martin Luther King, who responded to reprehensible treatment and hatred in a noble fashion that inspired millions and changed society. Our own responsibility may be smaller in scope, but in the cosmic scheme it is no less important. Each act of kindness has meaning.

Every time we respond to a difficult person, we have the potential to serve as an example to others of how to respond in a positive fashion.

Teaching a Difficult Person

Few things are harder to put up with than the annoyance of a good example.

MARK TWAIN

If we can teach others by example, then why not a difficult person as well? The answer is that we can, but only if we aren't trying to teach them.

One of the more offensive types of people on any interpersonal hit list is the kind who gives unsolicited advice. If I offer you advice without first getting your permission, I am sending you the message that you're dumb and I'm smart. It shouldn't be too surprising that such advice is usually not well received—no one likes feeling stupid. Sometimes we offer advice not to help but to make ourselves feel better.

Imagine how a difficult person might respond if you were to interact with her based on the spoken or unspoken assumption that she needed to learn something from you. Chances are, she wouldn't respond well.

Do difficult people come our way because they have something to learn from us? Perhaps. But we cannot improve the relationship if we operate from this assumption, because it creates a distorted connection. No relationship will improve if one of the parties considers himself superior and the other party isn't in agreement.

In order for us to teach a difficult person, we have to be subtle in our approach. The best thing to do is to not do anything. By just being ourselves we can hope that who we are and the example we set may have an effect on what the difficult person does.

During one of my workshops, a participant talked about how she wanted to improve her relationship with her "difficult" daughter. The woman was an avid spiritual seeker, regularly attending workshops on spiritual topics and reading books with spiritual themes. Her daughter wasn't spiritual; that, according to the woman, was the primary source of the difficulties.

I chose not to challenge the woman's perception of her situation because I sensed that she would not be receptive. But it seemed to me that even though the woman said the right things and held lofty spiritual beliefs, she wasn't living according to their principles. One expresses genuine spirituality primarily through action, not through belief. I strongly suspected that the woman was the greater contributor to the difficulties. She had a smug attitude that the daughter no doubt found offensive.

God may send difficult people to us so that we can teach them. But we need to teach through our humble example, not our self-righteous talk.

Difficult People Teach Us Empathy and Compassion for the Suffering of Others

No one may forsake his neighbor when he is in trouble. Everybody is under obligation to help and support his neighbor as he would like himself to be helped.

MARTIN LUTHER

I once knew a woman who literally had never been sick a day in her life. Her perfect health was a wonderful blessing for her but unfortunately not for others. It caused her to be unsympathetic to anyone else's illness; she would always assume those who claimed to be ill were just avoiding responsibility. Given the position of leadership she held, it made things very uncomfortable for her staff, who received no understanding or sympathy from her when they called in sick.

Then she went on a trip to a third-world country. After drinking the local water, her perfect health evaporated. She became bedridden with severe diarrhea; for the first time in her life, she was miserable and incapacitated.

But to her credit, she learned from the experience. From that point on, she understood what it was like to be sick and never accused anyone else of pretending again.

Illness became her teacher.

One of life's enduring truths is that we may only be able to appreciate the suffering of others when we have endured similar suffering ourselves.

Support groups are built on this very premise; only from fellow sufferers can we receive the heartfelt understanding and compassion that we need so badly during our trials. Only a cancer survivor can understand the terror of someone who has just been diagnosed. Only a widow can understand what it is like to lose one's husband.

If one obligation of being human is to help others, then suffering, however painful and unwelcome, prepares us to provide that help.

This book is about a particular type of suffering, the suffering we endure from other people. So let's be specific about their role in our lives as it relates to helping others. Through our encounters with difficult people, we are better able to understand and offer meaningful help to someone else who is undergoing similar difficulties.

For example, a woman who has endured and eventually left an abusive husband can provide invaluable support to someone still being abused. An employee who has learned over the years how to successfully deal with a tyrannical business owner can mentor new employees so that they do not have to suffer in the same fashion.

Our capacity to help others is enhanced each time we undergo an encounter with a difficult person. It is as if we are being prepared so that we can be ready when someone else needs our help.

Our suffering at the hands of difficult people prepares us to help others who are experiencing similar treatment.

Difficult People Let Us Know We're Loved

The love of our neighbor in all its fullness simply means being able to say to him, "What are you going through?"
S I M O N E   W E I L

When we experience mistreatment from a difficult person, we can feel beaten down and forlorn. This is a time to ask for help from those around us. Many people find there is a vast resource of love they can tap into when they need it, love that was never appreciated before.

After Mary's husband abruptly left her for another woman, her friends stayed with her around the clock until she began to calm down. After that they called, checked in frequently, invited her over, and let her know that she could rely on them at any time. She was overwhelmed by their loving support.

Sometimes, when troubles beset us, we withdraw from others instead of reaching out for help. Admitting that we need other people may be our spiritual lesson. The pain evoked by our encounters with difficult people can force us out of isolation so that we open our hearts.

Sometimes we receive reminders that we are loved when we are provided with an opportunity to receive love.

Difficult People Help Us to Develop Our Latent Qualities

We can't take any credit for our talents. It's how we use them that counts.

MADELEINE L'ENGLE

Tom and Frank got to know each other on their company softball team. After several years of talking about their dreams over beers after the games, they decided to leave their respective jobs and become business partners. Tom excelled at sales and marketing. Frank, who was more reserved, had an MBA, solid financial skills, and knew how to manage a business efficiently.

They dipped into their savings and took the plunge, starting out in Tom's family room to minimize expenses. Slowly, business grew. They got an office, hired more employees, and started to become players in their industry. Within three years, they were a success and the envy of those they had left behind at their previous jobs.

Once things started going well, Tom began to take the business less seriously. He came in late, left early, and took time off to be with his family or just play golf. This was irritating to Frank, who believed in hard work. He also worried that things could go downhill at any time for all sorts of unanticipated reasons.

The disagreements between them grew more intense, and they finally had a showdown. Tom insisted that his dream had always been to take it easy; Frank protested that Tom's leisure time was only possible because he himself worked so hard. They could not come to a mutually agreeable resolution of their philosophical difficulties, so Frank offered to buy out Tom's share of the business. With the help of attorneys and accountants, the deal was finalized.

Frank now owned the business, but that meant he had to learn all the things that Tom used to do. It was painful for him to deal with customers, something Tom had done easily. Eventually he overcame his shyness and his ability to generate new business blossomed. He realized he could have done it all himself from the very beginning if he'd had more self-confidence.

All of us are born with certain talents and abilities. Mathematics, language, and athletics are three that readily come to mind. But there are many others. Some people are naturally musical, while some can't hold a tune. Some people can create something delicious from scratch without a cookbook, while some couldn't exist without a microwave oven and a freezer full of frozen entrees. Each of us is good at doing some things and not good at others.

Our society tends to place high value on certain abilities and less on others, and our parents often have their own designs for our future. As we grow up, our teachers and parents steer us a certain way with the intention of developing our talents in the direction of society's values and their own agenda for us. But they don't always send us in the right direction, because talents are innate, not just learned. We might, for example, start music lessons at a young age because our parents think we should be able to play music, not because we are musical. By the time we become adults, some of our abilities have been developed through schooling, training, and practice; others, however, may remain dormant because they haven't been recognized or valued earlier in life. Alternately, because of our fears, we may have avoided expressing and developing them. Frank's fear of sales is a good example.

Difficult people can force us to develop these latent talents. By rising to the occasion, as Frank did, we may discover we are competent at doing something we previously avoided. Or we may find we have a talent that we didn't even know about. Difficult people can help us to become strong in the areas where we previously felt weak.

In order to rise to the challenge of dealing with a difficult person, we may be compelled to make use of latent talents and abilities that we need to develop.

Difficult People Impel Us to Action

Even pain
Pricks to livelier living.

AMY LOWELL

Karen, by anyone's standards, was not a good housekeeper. Household objects in her home had a tendency to mysteriously vanish under piles of miscellany. Newspapers were archaeological artifacts, preserved for eventual discovery in the distant future. Cans, bottles, jars, and other assorted containers were recyclable—someday.

Karen's husband Joe had long ago given up trying to straighten up the mess, since it increased faster than his efforts to remove it. Nevertheless he loved her, and he had become resigned to living this way. Nagging accomplished nothing.

His parents also loved Karen but found the apartment unpleasant to be in and avoided coming over if they could, with polite excuses. However, when Joe's aunt Margaret came to the United States for a visit from Germany, accompanied by her new husband Rolf, stopping by appeared to be unavoidable.

Upon arriving, Rolf, true to his German heritage of neatness and cleanliness, was blunt. "This is the filthiest apartment I've ever seen. How can you live like this?"

Karen began to cry, Joe was embarrassed, and the rest of the afternoon was strained. However, that evening, Karen confessed to Joe that she knew the place was in terrible shape and had wanted to start cleaning but felt paralyzed because the task seemed too immense. Joe offered to get friends to help and even enlisted his parents, who were happy to pitch in.

Rolf's rudeness was just what Karen needed to get moving.

All of us have made resolutions that we haven't kept and have postponed our self-improvement initiatives with weak excuses. We might procrastinate about going back to school, avoid dieting and exercise, or find reasons not to leave a job we dislike.

Some things in our life can be safely ignored. Others can't; if we continue to avoid giving such unpleasant tasks our attention, a difficult person might just step in for us. Sometimes an insult or unkind remark from someone can be upsetting enough to inspire us to change.

The Universe may send us difficult people to impel us to take needed action.

Difficult People Serve as Reminders

Experience isn't interesting till it begins to repeat itself—
in fact, till it does that, it hardly is experience.

ELIZABETH BOWEN

Paul hated criticism. Yet it seemed to follow him wherever he
went. He had critical teachers in school, critical bosses at work,
and critical girlfriends on dates. It seemed as if everybody was
always criticizing Paul, and he didn't understand why.

After he started seeing a therapist, he began to realize that he
was his own worst critic. Criticism, although painful, was familiar
and comfortable. Paul had grown up with a critical mother; criticism was a daily experience for him. After he moved away from
home, he continued to criticize himself. Somehow he drew critical
people into every sphere of his activity to reinforce his negative self-
image. Paul needed to do some work on the way he viewed himself,
replacing the negative self-lecturing with positive self-love.

If there are aspects of ourselves that are still unresolved, if
there are spiritual lessons yet unlearned, difficult people will be
drawn into our lives to bring them to our attention. And if one
difficult person doesn't seem to get through, others will keep
coming until we finally figure out the spiritual lessons that are
being presented.

If there is a consistent theme in the kinds of difficult people who
come into your life, they may be reminding you of the inner work
that you need to do. Pay attention.

Difficult People Help Us to Avoid Stagnation

The tragedy of life is that people do not change.

AGATHA CHRISTIE

Sandra and Robert, a couple in their preretirement years, had both lost their first spouses and found loving comfort in each other's embrace after several sad years of widowhood.

They lived in a seacoast village that drew a lively stream of tourists. For a number of years, Sandra ran a historic bed-and-breakfast there. The building was built in the 1830s and had a picturesque view of a lighthouse and harbor.

When the two married, she moved a mile inland to Robert's house but continued to operate the bed-and-breakfast, shuttling back and forth a number of times each day. After several years of this arrangement, they decided it would make sense to sell his house and expand hers. This way, they could live comfortably at the bed-and-breakfast, making it easier for her to attend to the needs of guests.

They contacted a prominent architect and drew up plans for a tasteful addition to the living quarters of the bed-and-breakfast that preserved the character of the neighborhood and addressed environmental concerns arising from its coastal location.

When the zoning board met, Sandra and Robert received a nasty jolt. The surrounding neighbors, who had said nothing until now, were vocal and united in opposing the remodeling plan. Their primary argument, that the addition would create more traffic and congestion, was without merit since the number of guest rooms would not be increasing. Nevertheless, the zoning board weighed the positive features of the plan against the strong neighborhood opposition and decided to turn it down.

These neighbors were people whom Sandra had known and been cordial with for as long as thirty years; they had raised their children together and done all of the things that good neighbors do. She had even given up lodging income from time to time in order to house her neighbor's visiting relatives without charge when they came to attend the children's weddings.

After the meeting, several uncharacteristic and threatening letters arrived from one next-door neighbor with whom they had had a warm and previously unblemished history. Their plans for a better life were being thwarted in an unanticipated and disheartening way.

Sandra and Robert were upset, disappointed, and angry, both at having their plans stymied and at the unpleasant and unexpected reactions of their neighbors. They thought about fighting the neighbors; they also considered building a smaller addition that would not require zoning board approval.

But after a good deal of agitation and contemplation, they both arrived at the same realization. Maybe it was time to move on, to explore other interests and pursue their passions. Retirement would be upon them in a few more years; maybe this was a signal for them to begin serious planning now instead of continuing to enjoy their current life as it was and waiting a while longer to ponder change. They began to see the situation as an opportunity to consider new options and possibilities that they hadn't entertained earlier.

When relationships that have previously been good suddenly go bad, it may be an indication that change is beckoning.

Most of us are creatures of comfort, with not a lot of incentive to make changes in our lives when things are going well. But sometimes we continue to remain in situations or relationships that have outlived their usefulness. Nothing is really wrong with our circumstances, but we're no longer growing and learning, and the Universe has other plans for us.

That's when a certain kind of difficult person enters the picture, someone who didn't used to be that way. Unknowingly, such people have been converted to a divine cause, the cause of our spiritual growth. Their change of heart precipitates our change of soul.

When people who haven't been a problem before suddenly become one, they may be serving as a catalyst for changes that we need to make or situations that we need to leave.

Difficult People Serve as Mirrors

Everyone is a moon, and has a dark side which he never shows to anybody.

MARK TWAIN

When Doria left her corporate job as a benefits specialist and began her own consulting firm, she spent most of her energy trying to generate clients. It was a numbers game; the more companies she contacted, the greater the possibility of finding work. Whenever a prospective client would call, all her time and hope would be focused in that direction until a contract resulted or the job failed to come to fruition.

One March morning, Doria received an excited, enthusiastic call from the human resources director at a rapidly growing telemarketing firm. He had received her marketing brochure, and she seemed to be offering exactly what he was looking for.

The two met, and he again indicated how interested he was in her consulting services. All he needed to do was to get the president's approval, and they could start.

That didn't happen right away. The president was out of town, he was too busy to meet, things were changing rapidly, and nothing could be done until the dust settled. Doria received continued assurances of strong interest—the human resources director promised to make bringing her proposal to the president's attention his top priority. Finally he did meet with the president. All that resulted was that the president asked for more information.

In the meantime, Doria kept her hopes up and spent time

doing additional research and writing a lengthy proposal, all without a consulting fee. Her frustration and annoyance grew. By fall, it was finally apparent that nothing was going to come of the initial contact.

Doria gave up, and by now she was angry. She was angry at the human resources director for the empty promises, for leading her on, and for telling her what she wanted to hear instead of giving her an honest assessment of the facts. And she was angry at herself for believing him.

Then Doria came to a realization that was even more painful than the disappointment of having her plans fall through and the discouragement of having wasted her time. What was so upsetting was the realization that what she disliked so much in the human resources director was something she did herself to other people.

One of Doria's blind spots was a tendency to tell people what they wanted to hear at the moment. Instead of speaking the truth, which she feared might disappoint, discourage, or cause people to dislike her, Doria would say whatever served her own interests without considering her impact on others. She made promises and told people things that would keep them involved and engaged with her even when she had little of substance to offer.

Other people had learned from repeated experience that Doria had this tendency. They steered clear of her or they accepted the fault and adjusted their expectations accordingly. Doria, however, was still largely unaware of her own tactics until she spotted them in the human resources director and slowly and painfully began to recognize them in herself.

What Doria discovered is that difficult people often serve as mirrors. They reflect our own flaws. What we don't like in another is often, but not always, something we don't like in ourselves.

All of us have parts of ourselves that we don't care for and don't care to look at. Because we find our imperfections so unappealing, and because most of us don't even like to admit we have them, we suppress them. We push them away and pay attention only to our good qualities.

But the more we try to push something out of our awareness, the more it will pop up. As psychiatrist Harold Bloomfield points out, what we resist persists.

So sometimes, when we look at another with distaste, we are really looking at the places inside ourselves that we have until now tried to evade. If we avoid looking inside, we will run into the very trait we are avoiding in other people.

If you are someone who wants to expand your self-knowledge, difficult people can provide you with a valuable source of information. Each time you meet someone with qualities you don't like, you receive potential clues about areas within yourself that you have ignored and that are demanding your attention.

Previously, we talked about the various skills that we possess, both expressed and latent, bestowed on us by God.

God has given us our flaws as well as our talents. One reason is that in the process of correcting them, we grow closer to holiness. But another, less obvious reason for our flaws is that they can be used to our advantage if they are acknowledged and properly applied.

I know someone named Gary who is extremely obstinate; when someone says no to him, it just inspires him to think of a new strategy to get a yes. Lots of people have found his persistence annoying, but on a number of occasions persevering in the face of opposition has served him well. Sometimes those who have opposed him have been wrong, and by overcoming their resistance he has ended up doing the right thing. On other occasions, his persistence has led to achievements that he might never have realized if he had just accepted someone's no and given up prematurely. Gary has turned his weakness into a strength.

Once I was complaining to my youngest brother about something my father had done. My brother sympathized but then pointed out to me that the qualities my brothers and I find so hard to take in my father are the very same qualities that enabled him to survive six years under the Nazis. If it weren't for the flaws I find so troubling in him, I wouldn't be here.

If our faults remain unknown to us, they invariably cause problems in our relationships because we are unaware of how we impact others; our unseen faults get in the way. But if our faults are known to us, we can act with awareness of our potential to be insensitive and actually leverage our shortcomings to our advantage.

Embracing our negative qualities in the same way that we value our positive ones is an important step toward self-knowledge. Difficult people can be an essential tool for uncovering these qualities. Finding them by ourselves is not something we are inclined to do and is not easy to do even if we are so inclined.

Difficult people are like mirrors that help to reveal our blind spots, the aspects of ourselves that we conceal. By taking ownership of our imperfections and bringing them into our conscious mind, we are able to use them positively in our lives.

Difficult People Help Us to Work on Our Character

Talent develops in quiet places, character in the full current of human life.
JOHANN WOLFGANG VON GOETHE

Passing an easy test in school doesn't demonstrate that a student has learned much. So it is with spiritual tests. The tougher the test, the greater the accomplishment.

Being helpful, generous, and kind to our friends, relatives, and those we are attracted to is easy. Acting that way comes naturally and spontaneously to us. Expressing the positive side of our character is something we enjoy doing for those we care about and for those who appreciate our goodwill.

But in the presence of a difficult person, these qualities are much harder to express. It is easy to be unkind, to lose our temper, to be withholding and vindictive when we have been mistreated. If we can express our positive side when someone else is being negative, we grow spiritually. We grow closer to and begin to emulate God, whose love is unconditional.

By learning how to control our anger, refrain from criticism, or cultivate patience, we become better people. The harder the challenge, the greater the achievement. We will explore this notion more fully in chapter 7.

Each difficult person makes it possible for us to work on refining our character.

Difficult People Help Us to Rectify the Distant Past

Finding myself to exist in the world, I believe I shall in some shape or other always exist; and, with all the inconveniences human life is liable to, I shall not object to a new edition of mine, hoping, however, that the "errata" of the last may be corrected.

BENJAMIN FRANKLIN

A recent Gallup Poll found that 27 percent of the adult population of the United States believes in the idea of reincarnation. The percentage is far higher in Asia and the Pacific Rim, where reincarnation is a central teaching of Hindu and Buddhist thought. Discussion about reincarnation is also found in the writings of Kabbalah, the mystical branch of Judaism, and early Christianity included the concept until it was later rejected.

Those who believe in reincarnation maintain there is a soul separate from the physical body that has inhabited other bodies in earlier lifetimes and will return again to do so in the future. Souls return to continue a learning process that spans many lifetimes. If a relationship during an earlier lifetime is unresolved, the two souls meet again to make another attempt at resolution.

For individuals who believe in reincarnation, difficult people are those with whom one has unfinished business from the distant past.

Difficult People Prepare Us for Future Challenges

The future enters into us, in order to transform itself in us, long before it happens.

RAINER MARIA RILKE

If we accept the existence of God, then it is logical to also accept the existence of a divine plan. God wouldn't be much of a Creator if things just happened randomly once they were set in motion.

A divine plan that encompasses all Creation, written by a Creator that created this vast universe, would have to include each of us. In other words, there would have to be a divine plan for each soul, a plan that unfolds throughout life, a plan that would be invisible since to know it would interfere with our free will to choose.

The plan would call for each soul to have certain experiences at certain times with certain people. Sometimes the people would be difficult, because for reasons that are unfathomable, the soul must learn from a particular person in preparation for an unknowable future. We saw earlier how a simple interaction between two people can have repercussions throughout life. It's all part of a plan.

Difficult people prepare us for the future in ways that we cannot understand in the present.

Living the Mystery

Be patient toward all that is unresolved in your heart and try to love the questions themselves *like locked rooms and like books that are written in a very foreign tongue. Do not now seek the answers, which cannot be given because you would not be able to live them. And the point is, to live everything.* Live *the questions now. Perhaps you will then gradually, without noticing it, live along some distant day into the answer.*

RAINER MARIA RILKE

If you are currently in the midst of unpleasant relationship difficulties, you may be tempted to choose one particular viewpoint in this chapter to explain your suffering. Try to resist the temptation, since there is no way of knowing the reasons for your travails. You don't want premature closure to hamper your further growth.

Each viewpoint is here to uplift and offer inspiration. My goal has been to convince you that spiritual forces are operating behind the scenes at every moment—your suffering is not a chance occurrence. Suffering serves as a means to accelerate your spiritual progress by shattering your complacency. Suffering is how the Universe gets your attention.

If God sends us difficult people, and the experience is agonizing for us, then we are tempted to blame God for our suffering. It is conceivable that God made a mistake. But more likely it is we who are mistaken; we are locked into viewing our circumstances in a way that keeps us miserable and doesn't extricate us from our suffering. With luck, the viewpoints presented in this chapter will illuminate some of the reasons why suffering exists in our relationships.

Live with the mystery. Accept your experiences with a difficult person and learn from them. You may never know the reasons why. Or perhaps one day the reasons for your suffering will come to you unbidden, once your difficulties have been resolved. By accepting the unknown, you are making room for something new in your life.

We can try to understand life's mysteries, but this is like trying to understand the undulations of a wheat field or the shape of a cloud. Opening our hearts to the mystery and meaning of our suffering can bring us into God's presence. Be grateful for this opportunity.

Explorations

LEARNING FROM OTHERS

Purpose: To cultivate the habit of learning from others

Each day, all sorts of people cross your path—at work, in public, at home, on television. Is it possible to observe them with an eye toward learning? Consider the following questions as a starting point:

- What are they good at doing?
- What mistakes do you observe them making?
- How well or badly do they treat other people?
- Do you like being treated the way they treat you?
- Do you treat other people this way?
- What qualities do they possess that you'd like to develop in yourself?
- What qualities do they possess that you'd like to eliminate in yourself?
- If more people were like them, would the world be a better place?
- If you were like them, would you be a better person?

The main idea is to start to make connections between what other people do and what you do as a way to turn your own behaviors in a positive direction.

REMEMBERING

Purpose: To enhance your appreciation of what others have done for or done to you and the lasting effects they've had

Step 1   Think back to a single incident in which someone did
          or said something that affected you positively for a long
          time afterward. It could have been a teacher, friend,
          parent, or stranger. On a piece of paper, make three
          columns. In the first column list the person's name, in
          the second what he or she said or did, and in the third
          how it affected you.

Step 2   Now try to think of others who had a positive effect
          on you. Add them to your list in the same fashion. At
          this point, if you wish, thank them silently. Or if you
          are so moved, write or call and let them know how
          much you appreciate what they did. It will make
          their day.

Step 3   After your list is done, try to put yourself in each per-
          son's shoes. Do you think the behavior was deliberate
          or spontaneous? Do you think the person realized at the
          time what the impact on you would be? Chances are,
          those people who affected you strongly probably acted
          purposefully but didn't realize what an impression they
          would leave.

Step 4   Now, take another piece of paper and create the same
          three columns. But this time list people who affected
          you negatively. What did they do, and how were you
          affected?

Step 5   Think about whether their behavior was deliberate or inadvertent. Do you think they had any idea how badly you felt afterward? In this case, it's more likely the behavior was unthinking and the effect unknown.

Note: If you are moved to call or write the people on this list, curb your inclination—it would serve no useful purpose right now other than to be hurtful. This does not mean you should suffer in silence, but there is a time and a place for this conversation, and you want to be prepared for it. Chapter 5 offers some suggestions for preparing yourself.

Step 6   Now, think about times when you've received feedback from someone telling you that you've had a powerful effect on that person either positively or negatively. Did you act intentionally? Were you aware at the time of how powerful your effect was?

Step 7   As a concluding step, think about the awesome responsibility of interacting with others. Through simple words or actions, people have affected you, and you've affected others. Consider also the fact that the incidents you thought of in step 6 only represent those you know about—how many others might there be that you don't know about?

THINKING BACK

Purpose: To consider the possibility that a particular difficult person is doing to you what you once did to someone else

If God wants us to learn how our behaviors affect others, what better way than to have someone do to us what we once did to someone else!

The process works best, of course, if one makes the connection between the present and the past. The purpose of this exercise is to help you do that.

Some years ago I was dating a woman who constantly criticized me. True to my own philosophy, I honestly asked myself if I ever did the same, and I was able to say at the time that I hadn't. At least until I found myself on the phone one day with my younger brother, criticizing his latest interest, using the same tone and attitude as the woman I was dating. I had been doing so for years without ever realizing it, and since I did it to only my brother, I wasn't able to see the connection right away between my girlfriend's behavior and my own.

So even though this exercise is very simple, it might take some time to come to fruition.

Think back and try to remember a time when you treated someone else the way you are being treated now. If no one comes to mind, it could mean that the Universe has sent the person to you for a different reason. Or it could mean that you haven't yet made the connection.

Meditation, prayer, and dreams can all help in making the connection. More will be said about these approaches in the next chapter.

If there is a connection to be made, you will know when you've made it—you will have a moment of recognition and insight that is unmistakable. Be patient in waiting for that moment to come.

I'll Never Do That!

Purpose: To recall past incidents that have inspired you to not act a certain way toward others

Think of people in your past who have set the worst example. These are the people whose behavior you have found the most painful and unpleasant. Now consider whether your current set of behaviors is a reaction to theirs.

Step 1   One possibility is that you are doing the opposite of what they did to you. This is good if you learned from the experience and now act appropriately—for example, if your parents had no time for you and you give your children lots of attention, or if they constantly screamed at you and you are careful to raise your voice only when the situation warrants it.

Step 2   Consider also whether you have gone too far to the other extreme. If, for example, your parents were obsessed with money, are you someone who doesn't deal responsibly with money in return? If your parents were very religious and rigid about their beliefs, have you abandoned your own spirituality? If your art teacher criticized you, are you now someone who refuses to do anything artistic?

Step 3   Consider whether you have responded to a difficult person in your past by becoming like them. Often this happens without our realizing it. Think about whether your current behaviors echo those of someone in your past. If so, recall how painful it was for you and think about what it must feel like to those at the receiving end. Can you change?

A New and Improved You

Purpose: To recognize how meeting the challenge of a difficult person forces you to express talents that have been hidden or unexpressed

Make a list of the difficult people in your life, past and present; if you did the Taking Inventory exercise in chapter 1, then your list is partially done.

Now think about what you had to do to rise to the challenge each person presented. What aspects of yourself did you have to express? What did you discover about yourself in the process of dealing with each person that you didn't realize before? How are you different as a result of each encounter?

You may find that some of these difficult people have given you the gift of yourself. They have helped uncover a part of you that was previously dormant.

HERE WE GO AGAIN!

Purpose: To recognize patterns in your past interaction with difficult people

Go back to the Taking Inventory exercise in chapter 1 and complete it if you haven't already.

What patterns did you identify? Has God been teaching you the same lesson through different people? What is that lesson? What are you supposed to be learning?

If the same thing happens over and over to you, it's pretty clear that the Universe is trying to get your attention.

MIRROR, MIRROR ON THE WALL, WHO'S THE MOST DIFFICULT OF THEM ALL?

Purpose: To cultivate the habit of looking within when you find something you dislike in another person

Go back to the Taking Inventory exercise in chapter 1 and complete it if you haven't already. The column on the far right describes the negative traits that the difficult people in your life possess.

Be absolutely honest. How many of them describe you?

If you haven't identified at least one, either you are perfection in a human body or you aren't yet aware of some of your own negative traits.

In your daily life, when you find yourself disliking a trait in someone else, stop and ask yourself if you also possess that trait. You may be surprised to find the answer is yes more often than you would like to admit.

PART II

HEALING
THE
DIFFICULTIES

CHAPTER 5

HEALING FROM WITHIN

Healing Difficult Relationships

Relationships that do not end peacefully, do not end at all.
MERRIT MALLOY

Each week, Charlie waits in his car at the end of the block like a cop on a stakeout when it comes time to pick up his son; he and his former wife still can barely stand to say hello to each other, even though the divorce has been final for years.

Derek is now a regular at the Irish bar with the large green shamrocks on the window. Even before he starts drinking, Derek still speaks bitterly to anyone who will listen about the boss who fired him capriciously from a high-paying job after ten years of faithful service.

Susan was utterly startled and felt physically ill when she spotted her former best friend with her former boyfriend at the local Thai restaurant. They'd been married for some time, had moved to another city, and she thought she'd finally gotten over it.

Kristen wonders if she'll ever get over her feelings toward Greg, the man who beat her regularly and from whom she had to flee to a hidden shelter for battered women. She thinks about him

145

every time she looks in the bathroom mirror and sees the scar on her cheek.

Andy hasn't spoken to his parents in twenty-three years, ever since he got married to his college sweetheart who came from a different religious background and his parents disowned him. He tried to visit his father in the hospital before his father passed away, but his mother had left strict instructions with the nursing staff that no one could visit her husband without her permission. He was ignored at the funeral.

People do terrible things to each other. Relationships are ripped apart, and though there's often no physical harm, the psychic damage is even more long lasting and painful. All of us have unfinished business. We have difficult relationships in the present, and we have relationships from the past that are unresolved. How do we heal? How do we finish our unfinished business? Is it possible to arrive at a place of resolution with a difficult person?

Healing unfinished business is one of our most important spiritual tasks. Unfinished business stays that way until we do something to resolve it, even though it may no longer operate at a conscious level. It lingers and eventually must be addressed, like a financial debt that eventually must be paid. If the ultimate spiritual lesson is love, anything less means that there is still work to do.

A relationship can be considered unfinished if it still possesses an uncomfortable emotional component and if we still expect something from the other party. If our feelings are still loaded, it's not over for us. If we still want the other person to do or say whatever will right the wrong, it's not over. That's true even if we'd like to think it's over and even when one party has left and we no longer have contact.

Sheila came to one of my workshops to deal with her sister Geri. For years Geri had criticized Sheila, and Sheila finally had had enough. She announced one day to Geri that she would no longer have anything to do with her and felt an enormous sense of relief at her bold act.

Subsequently, when Sheila would run into Geri at family events, she would say a very cursory hello and then try to pretend Geri wasn't there. Geri, however, kept trying to get Sheila's attention, since she still wanted a relationship. Sheila had come to the workshop to try to get Geri to leave her alone—she just wanted Geri out of her life. She thought that by making a unilateral decision to cut off her sister, she could consider the problem solved.

I didn't need to tell Sheila that things weren't yet finished with her sister because the other workshop participants said it for me. Sheila's solution might help on a day-to-day basis, preventing her sister's verbal attacks, and if she wanted to punish Geri she was doing so successfully, but the deeper issues between the sisters weren't being addressed. Avoidance is not the same as healing.

While it is easy to define unfinished business, it is not so simple to define healing in the context of a relationship. Healing is more than feeling better, more than a conversation about differences, more than the cessation of conflict, and more than the resumption of civil behavior. Healing can be gradual or it can come in a cathartic moment. Healing can take place with or without the other party's involvement. It is an internal process, not an external event.

In essence, healing is a recognition that whatever difficulties existed no longer exist. It is lightness, release, and ease in place of intensity, pain, and preoccupation. It is letting go of all expectations regarding the other person. It is learning the spiritual lessons that brought the difficulties into your life. Ultimately, it involves forgiveness.

It is always preferable to deal with unfinished business and heal the relationship with the other person's participation, because this method has the potential to bring the deepest healing, a combination of forgiveness and reconciliation. But to achieve a satisfactory resolution, inner preparation is necessary—think of it as intraper-sonal homework. One needs to approach the other person from a place of insight and emotional balance, and until one has arrived at that place by doing the necessary inner work, the outcome will not be entirely satisfactory.

Sometimes it just isn't possible or prudent to talk to a person, and the healing must take place alone. This chapter offers a num-ber of approaches for beginning the process of healing without the involvement of the other person, whether as preparation for a face-to-face discussion or because one isn't feasible.

There are several scenarios in which healing alone is the only option. Sometimes the other person might be violent, and a con-frontation could lead to physical harm. Other times, the person refuses to cooperate despite repeated efforts. On occasion, the other person may live somewhere else and not be easily accessi-ble. And people die, making reconciliation impossible.

> **We need four things to reach a level of comfort and release if there is unfinished business to resolve. First, a desire for healing. Second, the courage to experience the unpleasant emotions that inevitably arise. Third, the willingness to acquire self-knowledge. And fourth, practical techniques.**

The Desire to Heal

> *Everyone says forgiveness is a lovely idea, until they have something to forgive.*
>
> C. S. Lewis

A desire to heal is a precondition if healing is to take place. A rela-tionship doesn't get better until at least one of the parties wants it to. Then why do people resist healing? Why do relationship diffi-culties linger? There are a number of possibilities.

• Some people can't be bothered or have more important things on their mind. Life goes on—they no longer care about something that happened a while back, even if it did end uncomfortably and relations are strained or nonexistent.

• Staying focused on the difficulties is a convenient way to avoid dealing with other important issues in one's life.

• A person might be avoiding the feelings that could come up if the difficult person were confronted. Dealing with the difficulties would mean feeling the emotions connected to the hurt in a deep and intense way. One may not be ready for that and might not be able to handle it.

• Some people paradoxically take comfort in their difficulties. By complaining to friends or a therapist, they get sympathy; if there is nothing to complain about, they fail to get the attention they crave.

• Not healing the difficulties is a way to punish the other person.

• Perpetuating the difficulties enables connections to be maintained. Discord and disharmony may be preferable to no relationship at all.

• If someone experienced lots of conflict growing up, then difficulties in a relationship will be viewed as the normal way of relating to another; harmony will be unknown and unfamiliar.

• Refusing to heal is a way to keep the relationship on one's own terms; one remains in control as long as one continues to withhold a willingness to reconcile.

• For some people, negative feelings are so familiar that they continue to hold on to anger or shame just to feel alive. The alternative is to have feelings that are unfamiliar and therefore uncomfortable.

• Some people feel that they deserve to suffer and be unhappy. Healing relationship difficulties would mean letting go of their attachment to misery and accepting the possibility that they deserve happiness.

• By holding on to negative feelings about a difficult person, one can maintain the illusion of superiority. The person wronged gets to feel righteous while the perpetrator is seen as the wrongdoer. The person wronged may also view him or herself as an innocent victim, while the perpetrator is cast as the evildoer. If the relationship is healed, the victim can't remain on the pedestal any longer.

• Some people get a sense of self from their hurt. As an incest survivor or the spouse of an alcoholic, they have a group to identify with and other people with whom to share their pain. If they let go of their hurt, they let go of who they think they are.

• People may be too proud to heal. Healing may imply that they have also contributed to the difficulties and require them to admit to themselves and others that they were wrong.

• Healing in its essence is self-knowledge. Those who resist looking within will resist healing.

• People may not know how to heal. They may be stuck in their feelings and not know what to do with them. They may not know what to say when they approach the difficult person.

• One may, inaccurately, see no hope of healing. Where there is no apparent chance of reconciliation, one is discouraged from the pursuit of healing.

> **Before a difficult relationship can be healed, one needs to look within, recognize the obstacles, and be willing to let go of them.**

How Deep Is the Hurt?

There are hurts so deep that one cannot reach them or heal them with words.

KATE SEREDY

Every unpleasant encounter with a difficult person creates emotional pain. After all, that's our definition of a difficult person— someone whose behavior evokes unwanted feelings.

Some encounters are worse than others. The mild ones bother us for a while, but eventually the feelings go away. The really difficult ones linger for a lifetime and can harden into permanent resentment and hatred.

To heal the feelings that don't just go away, we need to address the hurt that causes the pain. But why is it that some encounters hurt us so much more than others?

The first thing to consider is the duration of the difficulties. Is this a one-time occurrence, or has it been going on for a while? The longer the problem has existed, the deeper the hurt.

Second, we need to identify what we have lost. Difficult people always take something we value. If a stranger cuts us off in traffic, we just lose a minute or two of commuting time and some peace of mind. But if we have an accident because of another's poor driving, we may lose our health and our mobility. Other difficult people can take our reputation, our money, or our ideas; they can cause a loss of trust or safety. A difficult person can even, through betrayal or abandonment, cause us to lose our belief that the world is safe. So the greater the loss of something we value, the greater the pain.

Third, we need to look at the nature of our relationship with a difficult person. Losses caused by strangers are bad; losses caused by someone we are close to can be staggering. Our expectations are so much higher of those we love—partners, siblings, and parents; correspondingly, the pain we experience when they hurt us is that much greater. This is why incest causes the deepest wounds—it constitutes the greatest betrayal by the people one trusts the most.

Fourth, how are we wounded? Our own emotional wounds from the past play an important role in how difficult people affect us. Certain behaviors may be much more devastating because they trigger old, buried hurts that have never healed.

Fifth, what is our present ability to deal with emotional pain?

Are we mature? Physically healthy? Have we done inner work to heal our old wounds from childhood? How much insight do we possess into ourselves? What strengths do we have? Who is there to give us love and support if we need it? If our mental, physical, emotional, and spiritual selves are healthy, then difficult people will not affect us as deeply. For the majority of situations, our inner resources will enable us to deal with the situation and protect us from lasting harm. We will be able to let go of the hurt and move on.

Difficult people hurt us. But the intensity of our hurt is not determined just by their behavior. It also depends on us.

Experiencing Intense Emotions

A man who has not passed through the inferno of his passions has never overcome them.

C. G. JUNG

Our encounters with difficult people can bring up intense emotions—some of the most intense emotions we can experience. The reason we want so desperately to do something about these difficulties is because our feelings are so intolerable. Violence is one consequence of the inability to handle these strong feelings.

Much of the time, our tendency is to blame someone else for what we're feeling. After all, these feelings didn't come up until the other person came along.

But no one else is responsible for the feelings that we have. They are ours and ours alone. We might look at someone else as the cause, but this is just a distraction from the turmoil inside us. A difficult person may have done something awful, but that person didn't implant the feelings we're having into our head and heart.

Our intense feelings arise from our buried emotional wounds. To heal a relationship with another person, we need to heal our relationship with ourselves.

This type of healing is a lifelong process. It is the hardest work we can ever do because it requires facing our deepest hurts and fears. But because healing brings freedom, doing this inner work results in the greatest of rewards. By healing old wounds, we are freed from the self-created confinement of our own emotional reactivity.

Emotional pain, paradoxically, is good, because the worse it is, the more we are motivated to make necessary changes in our life.

The starting point for healing is deceptively simple. It merely requires that we not run away from ourselves; that we allow our intense emotions to stay in our awareness and be experienced. This is something very few of us know how to do, because we never learned how. Growing up, we watched our parents and others deal with their feelings a certain way, and we learned to do the same. We saw people holding their feelings inside, or denying altogether that they were angry or hurt or sad. We saw people distracting themselves with mind-numbing activities. And we saw people acting out their feelings through harsh words or cruel actions.

To break the habit, we need to learn how to stay with our discomfort. We need to stop pretending everything is fine. We need to learn to avoid the inappropriate use of crutches like alcohol, drugs, food, shopping, gambling, or television as a distraction or numbing balm. And we need to realize that in the long term it serves no useful purpose for us to blame, accuse, or attack another person because of what we are feeling, even though it might make us feel better at the moment.

One way to think about the process is to envision a rodeo with a bucking bronco. The rodeo star has one objective—to stay on the horse, no matter what. If he stays on, he can't get hurt—it's only by falling off that he may suffer a broken neck.

So it is with intense feelings. Paradoxically, even though every instinct in us wants to run from our emotions, we instead need to allow ourselves to feel the pain—to stay on the "emotional horse" to the extent we are able. Feelings, however intense and uncomfortable they might become, can't hurt us by being experienced.

It's when we don't feel them that we get into trouble. When we deny or suppress feelings, or don't express them in healthy ways, our physical health and capacity to enjoy life eventually deteriorate. When we distract ourselves from our feelings, we run the risk of becoming addicts, since an addiction is an unhealthy relationship with something (alcohol, drugs, food, money, gambling) used to reduce or avoid emotional pain. And when we act on our intense feelings, we run the risk of harming others and thereby ourselves.

By learning to fully experience what we're feeling, we can come to realize that feelings are not something we are, they are something we *have*. Their grip on us will gradually loosen.

The gateway to healing is feeling.

Spiritual Anesthesia

You cannot make yourself feel something you do not feel, but you can make yourself do right in spite of your feelings.
PEARL BUCK

Paradoxically, spiritual beliefs can present an obstacle to healing. To deal with difficult people spiritually, most of us already think we know what to do. We think that spiritual traditions teach us to be kind, to turn the other cheek, and to forgive.

These are always lofty ideals, but often lame advice. One can't be kind if one is still angry. One can't just turn the other cheek if an insult still stings. One can't forgive if one is filled with indignation and outrage at something a difficult person has done. It's very hard to act one way and feel another.

Spirituality does not mean pretending everything is fine when it isn't. It is not spiritual to act as if one has not been hurt when one has. It is unhealthy to suppress anger. It's not realistic to try to detach from emotional pain in the name of spirituality and rise above it.

If we want to take a spiritual approach, it means we must accept and feel our feelings, no matter how painful, and work with them to transform them. The spiritual part comes not in pretending we are okay, but in taking great care to not inflict pain on another regardless of what we're feeling and no matter what has been done to us.

Spirituality flows from what we do, not what we feel. Exercising restraint in spite of feeling deeply hurt is a laudable spiritual act. Trying to act as if something doesn't bother us when it does is spiritual anesthesia.

As a by-product of spiritual anesthesia, consider the following consequence. If you deny the intensity of your feelings in a relationship with another person in the name of spirituality, you may also be inhibiting your capacity to feel the intensity of your relationship with God.

We are not responsible for what we feel. We are responsible for what we do.

Using Physical Activity to Release

All emotions are, in essence, impulses to act.
DANIEL GOLEMAN

Feelings reside in our bodies as biochemical reactions. If we were to pay close attention during moments of emotional intensity, we would observe internal physiological changes in ourselves. Anger, for example, increases our heart rate and blood flow. Our fists and jaw clench, preparing us for dynamic action. When humiliated, we blush, and our head hangs down.

Since feelings are physical, physical activity is important for their release. Different parts of the body tend to accumulate emotional energy, depending on the emotion and the person.

Experiment to see which of the following approaches is helpful to you.

Mouth and Throat Certain movie scenes remain in my memory long after I've seen the movie and forgotten everything else. One example is a scene from the movie *Cabaret* in which Sally Bowles screams at the top of her lungs to get out her frustrations while a train is passing by. Screaming is a wonderfully therapeutic way to release feelings. The catch is finding a place to do it that doesn't embarrass you or disturb others. Try screaming in a parked car with the windows closed in the far corner of a parking lot. Or scream in a subway station while a train is going by. Acceptable public arenas for screaming include amusement parks and certain sporting events.

Singing is a less dramatic and more aesthetic way to release feelings orally.

If you tend to be verbally aggressive, talking back to a television, making nasty remarks while watching a video, or talking to a dead telephone will allow you to express your frustration.

Eyes Scientists have found that when tears are shed for emotional reasons, they have a different chemical make-up than they do when the eyes are simply irritated. Crying is a natural mechanism for the release of emotion. People who can't or won't cry are not taking advantage of an important emotional outlet.

Hands and Arms Physical activity using the hands and arms is another way to discharge emotional energy. Racquetball is a particularly effective sport since it requires smashing a ball as hard as one can. Chopping wood is a way to get work done at the same time as expressing feelings. Using a punching bag or a pillow or an encounter bat (a large, heavily padded club) can release hostility without harming anyone or anything. Throwing darts is a more social form of release. Snowball, water-balloon, and squirt-gun fights are fun ways to express aggression. If you feel the need to be destructive, try going to a recycling site and throwing glass bottles.

Feet and Legs Soccer, kick boxing, walking, biking, stair climbing, and running are all ways to discharge emotions locked in the lower part of the body.

Full Body Practicing a martial arts discipline is one of the best all-around ways to discharge negative feelings. You get to scream, hit, and kick in a context that is aggressive yet socially acceptable.

Also helpful are dancing, swimming, rowing, rock climbing, and cross-country skiing, which also involve the whole body.

Engaging in physical activity has another advantage in addition to emotional release. If we have a strong, healthy body, we are more resilient and can handle future encounters with difficult people more easily.

Despite these benefits of physical activity, there is an important point that needs to be made—while it is helpful, it does not address the source of the difficulties and is not a substitute for a face-to-face discussion.

It is important to have a nondestructive physical outlet for the expression of emotions.

Using the Body to Heal

The soul organizes the body as an expression of itself, as its instrument, as its intermediary with the world outside.

JOHN TERNUS

Physical activity is one useful way to vent the emotions that are currently troubling us. But as mentioned in chapter 3, we also suffer from buried emotional wounds acquired earlier in life that have never healed. We need a method to release these as well, or difficult people in the present will continue to trigger old hurts from the past.

Psychotherapy is the traditional approach for exploring the traumas of the past, and later in this chapter we'll discuss its value in healing relationship difficulties. There is, however, a limitation to the efficacy of talk therapy. Our emotional wounds aren't just in our minds; they are also in our bodies. Given that emotions are mediated by biochemical responses, when we experience traumatic emotions there must be some sort of lasting physiological impact. Physical activity and talk won't necessarily release it.

So let's consider three different ways of releasing emotional trauma from the body: bodywork, breathwork, and focusing. These may be unfamiliar to you; their value has only just begun to be recognized in the past few years.

Bodywork As we've pointed out, each time we experience an emotion, our body has a corresponding reaction. Negative and traumatic emotional experiences leave lasting imprints in the body, particularly in the fascia, the network of connective tissue that supports all the body's organs, muscles, and bones. It is as if the body creates an "armor" to protect itself from further assault.

Consider the plight of a young child who has a traumatic experience at the hands of an adult, such as a spanking or verbal humiliation. The child has not yet developed the capacity to defend herself physically or verbally. So the child's body is the only thing she has for protection against the pain of her own emotions and the unpredictable and threatening world outside. Now imagine yourself as that child, and consider how your own body must have responded.

One way to release our deeper emotional wounds, the ones

that can't be reached through physical activity or intellectual insight, is to work at the level of the body armoring that we have acquired over a lifetime. A trained bodyworker can read a person's emotional history through the sense of touch and can peel off the layers of accumulated armor.

Bodywork differs from traditional massage therapy. The latter is relaxing and releases surface stress. Bodyworkers, in contrast, have additional training that enables them to go deeper to locate and release the buried emotional traumas locked in the body. Receiving bodywork may not be as pleasurable as a traditional massage. The bodyworker's technique is more intense. Sometimes old emotions are reexperienced as they are released.

Breathwork The changes in our biochemistry that occur when we're under emotional stress are accompanied by changes in our breathing. Our breaths become shallower, and when we are startled we literally gasp, holding our breath from fear.

It made sense for our ancestors to be silent in the face of danger so predators could not locate them. The reflex to stop breathing at times of peril is an evolutionary mechanism designed to protect us from harm. But the dangers we face in modern society rarely require us to freeze in our tracks.

Breathwork is based on the premise that if breathing changes automatically in response to a stressful experience, then specific breathing techniques can be employed to recover from stress.

Focusing Every emotion has a corresponding physical correlate. If you say that you're feeling anxious, you only know this because your body is somehow telling you so. If you feel afraid, there is something going on inside you, something unclear, that you identify as fear. If you feel angry, you know it because you are picking up subtle telltale responses that your body has experienced as anger in the past.

Focusing was developed by Eugene Gendlin, a psychology professor at the University of Chicago. After years of investigation he discovered that the people who benefited the most from psychotherapy were those who were able to contact and work with their internal bodily awareness. Subsequently, he began teaching the process as a self-help tool that can be used independently of psychotherapy.

Focusing, in essence, is a technique for listening to your body and figuring out what it is telling you. Your body has much wisdom and provides lots of nonverbal clues about what is going on in your life. Focusing teaches you how to interpret them. Successfully tuning in to how the body is carrying a feeling or event results in a shift, an "aha" experience that indicates you have understood and experienced a degree of release regarding the issue being addressed.

Resources that provide more detailed information about each of these healing approaches are presented in the Notes section at the end of this book. The Explorations section at the end of this chapter contains an exercise to promote body awareness.

To heal the deeper emotional traumas that are buried in the body, it is helpful to make use of body-oriented approaches.

Healing Through Self-Knowledge

Wherever we go, whatever we do, self is the sole subject we study and learn.

RALPH WALDO EMERSON

Earlier in this book, we talked about the essence of difficult relationships—that our adversaries are our teachers. They teach us what we would fail to otherwise learn. Healing difficult relationships is therefore not just about emotional release, it is also about learning. And the lesson we need to learn is always about us.

To heal any difficult relationship we need to acquire self-knowledge. If we strive to learn the lessons that the Universe is sending us, then our difficulties ease because we no longer need an adversary to serve as a mirror for us. We don't need someone else to bring things to our attention.

Carl and Toni, both divorced and childless, lived in Seattle. They dated for several years, and while there was a lot of compatibility, things were often rocky between them. Carl had an unpleasant habit of pointing out Toni's supposed shortcomings whenever they encountered problems. He told her when she was being immature and self-centered. He pointed out when she was being controlling and manipulative. He asserted that she didn't consult him when she made decisions that affected both of them.

When Toni, who was undergoing a career crisis, ended up precipitously leaving her job as a manager at a large insurance company and started to experience money problems, Carl didn't show as much sympathy as Toni would have liked. When she could no longer afford her expensive apartment with a view of Puget Sound and had to economize with a smaller place, he offered irritating lectures about fiscal responsibility instead of being supportive about her loss. While he did take her out to eat, loaned her small amounts of money, and bought her clothes, he was impatient about her lack of direction and her financial irresponsibility.

Despite the criticism, Toni loved Carl and kept trying to make things work. She believed that he had her best interests at heart and that his opinions and observations of her were mostly accurate. She was constantly trying to do things to make him happy. Carl loved Toni as well; he enjoyed her lively personality and liked sharing and discussing life with her.

Things started to shift when Toni, who still had insurance coverage from her previous job, began to see a therapist, who encouraged her to look within. She learned to practice focusing and also to meditate and analyze her dreams. Through focusing, Toni became familiar with her body's reactions when she was not being treated with respect or when she was not acting with integrity. Through meditation, she became calmer inside so that Carl's criticisms didn't cause such instantaneous reactions on her part. And by analyzing her dreams, she came to see how she had not been expressing important aspects of her creativity. She could now view her unemployment as a gift that enabled her to change her focus to find her true vocation.

After doing inner work for a period of time, Toni slowly began to become more responsible financially and to be more realistic in the choices she made. She moved in new career directions. She saw where Carl had been accurate in some of his feedback; she also realized that his perceptions could have constructive effects. At the same time, she set limits to protect herself from his caustic side. But most importantly, she now recognized that if she could look at herself honestly, it would be less necessary for Carl to serve that purpose.

Difficult people are in our lives for a reason. Sometimes they help us to learn about ourselves, work on difficult issues, and confront painful truths.

Meaning and Feeling

The Truth must dazzle gradually
Or every man be blind.

EMILY DICKINSON

Healing, to summarize what we've said so far in this chapter, requires that we both work on our feelings and search for the spiritual meanings behind our difficulties. But these two are not separate—it is through feeling that we find meaning.

This last statement may seem like a paradox, since our habit is to use our intellect to understand the meaning of something. Here, however, the type of meaning that we are after is inner knowing. It is the quest for deeper personal truth rather than some abstract intellectual principle. It is an intuitive insight into ourselves that we haven't previously realized.

Our feelings can deliver us to this place of meaning. The very intensity of our feelings in a difficult relationship can show us the places inside that are hurt and crying out for attention. Negative feelings are indicators that something inside us has been neglected. They are signposts of a deeper, unfulfilled longing for spiritual sustenance. When we come to realize what it is within us that we've been evading or avoiding or ignoring or protecting, we have taken the first step toward finding spiritual meaning and healing our difficulties.

Dan and Richard worked together closely for several years, and Dan was devastated when his rival received the managerial promotion he sought. The promotion would have meant more money, more prestige, and more visibility; by not getting it he felt all these had been taken from him. The following days and weeks at work for him were filled with anger, resentment, disappointment, and depression. While Richard was friendly and gracious, Dan felt that behind the smile Richard was gloating.

Dan, unable to deal with his feelings, began to see a therapist. After a while he started to understand that his anger came from not getting the recognition he felt he deserved. He was then able to connect the anger to a troubled relationship with an older brother, who had received most of the attention in the family when they were growing up. Unconsciously, Dan had been directing the old, unhealed anger he carried toward his brother at Richard.

Further insight came when Dan realized that his identity was so overwhelmingly invested in his job that his other roles as father, husband, community member, churchgoer, and son were being neglected. By his losing the promotion, his desire to strengthen his identity and feel better about himself through work had been thwarted. He didn't yet know how to integrate the other pieces of his life to cultivate a more balanced and fulfilled sense of self.

Dan started to become more involved in church activities. Through study groups, he came to see that his longing for money and prestige were, in essence, desires that could never be satisfied, since the more he acquired, the more he would want. Having a primary relationship with material things and status was an attempt to compensate for his inability to gain richness and satisfaction from his relationships with people. Ultimately, Dan was able to acknowledge that his spiritual lesson was to work on his relationships, learning how to love and be loved.

Dan's process evolved over several years. He found meaning only because he was in so much pain that he was compelled to be receptive to new ways of looking at his life. Had he received the coveted promotion, he would have continued on the same ultimately empty course. By tracing the pain back to its source, he eventually found the deeper spiritual meanings that were hidden in his original difficulties with his coworker.

Finding spiritual meaning in our difficulties is an elusive process. It requires time and effort. Above all, it requires desire. But if we sincerely search for meaning, it will eventually come to us.

Different methods work for different people. Dan, for example, benefited from therapy. Toni, in the previous story, also used focusing, meditation, and dreamwork. The rest of this chapter describes various approaches, both psychological and spiritual, that can help you with your feelings and uncover the meaning of difficulties in your life.

Deep within your difficulties, beyond your intense feelings, are spiritual truths about your life.

Writing Down Your Feelings

The writer writes in order to teach himself, to understand himself, to satisfy himself.

ALFRED KAZIN

To write is to make concrete what is uncertain, abstract, and tentative. Feelings, impressions, and thoughts swirl around inside us as we encounter difficult people. Writing takes the swirling and makes it into visible letters and words that have meaning and focus.

By writing about difficult people, we take what's inside and fling it outside to behold and ponder. Our feelings, painful and unwanted, flow invisibly through our hands and fingers. They often are so eager to tell a story that they move with fury and purpose.

Writing heals. It both expresses feeling and fosters self-understanding. Writing is an outlet, a means of purging, a way to privately and safely damn those who make our lives so terribly difficult.

Writing has saved me many times from making nasty phone calls. It has kept me from saying the awful things that I wanted to say in the moment, barbed words that would have lingered in the heart of the listener like fishhooks. Instead of calling, instead of talking, I wrote it all down. I got it out. I screamed on paper, pounded my keyboard, talked to the screen, stayed up late. Exhausted, I finally went to bed and dreamed more acrimony.

Some of the things I've written to the people who have hurt me have taken weeks to put down in words because it took that long until the feelings subsided. But if I hadn't written my feelings out, I might have been poisoned by the toxicity of my own emotions for many months.

There are two ways to view writing in the context of a difficult relationship. You can write to get your feelings out, to understand your difficulties, and to feel better. Or you can write to communicate with the other person. It is crucial to recognize that you cannot do both with the same piece of writing. If you write to heal, the writing must be for your eyes only. It can be a serious mistake to share a letter written for yourself with a difficult person. The relationship could be irreparably damaged.

Several writing exercises to help with your intense feelings and to acquire insight into your difficulties can be found in the Explorations section of this chapter. In the next chapter we'll discuss writing as a form of communication with a difficult person.

Writing is a potent way to heal intense feelings and to acquire a greater understanding of the difficulties.

Talking to Someone About the Difficulties

The more we love our friends, the less we flatter them; it is by excusing nothing that pure love shows itself.

M O L I È R E

An acquaintance with a checkered work history had an ongoing problem with his current boss. He knew my background in management education and consulting, so when he spotted me at a social gathering, he approached me, wanting advice. What he really wanted was a sympathetic ear to confirm what an awful boss he had. I did listen sympathetically but also delicately pointed out some of the possible (in my mind probable) ways he might be (was) contributing to the difficulties through his own actions. The feedback did not go over well. I came to wonder if I had done the right thing by being so frank.

When we are having problems with someone, we often talk with our friends or family members about the difficulties, unless of course they are the difficult people. Our primary goal is to have someone validate our thoughts and feelings; we want another to confirm that we were indeed treated badly. By getting support from someone else, we are secretly hoping to hear that our nasty treatment is an anomaly and the rest of the world does indeed care about us. And, before we do something stupid, it's usually smart to check with somebody about our contemplated next step.

An important additional benefit of talking about our problems is that it lets us listen to ourselves. This can often lead to insights about the difficulties that we haven't had before. And it can serve as a vital means of expressing and venting emotion that doesn't hurt anyone.

The ingredient often missing in talking about our problems with friends is objective feedback. Sometimes we don't want to hear what we need to. Remember, in chapter 1 we pointed out that our perception of the difficulties is only one of several. To the extent ours is incomplete or inaccurate, we perpetuate the problem and fail to learn from it. There are times when the best of us create our own difficulties and then blame the problem on others.

In the story that began this section, I took it upon myself to point out a few blind spots to the person who asked for my advice. It may not have been the right time to do it; I may not have been the right person to do it. Nonetheless, all of us can benefit from this sort of feedback. Otherwise, we just keep doing what we've been doing, making the same mistakes over and over.

A good friend will listen to us without judgment, accept the intensity of our feelings, respect our pain, and express concern. A really good friend will, in addition, help us to see our situation in a new way.

Individual Therapy

We do not deal much in facts when we are contemplating ourselves.

MARK TWAIN

Some years ago a single friend in his late twenties moved back in with his parents after having lived on his own since college. He was making preparations to move to Brazil on a potentially lengthy work assignment, his apartment lease was up, and he wanted to spend some time with them before he left.

Once he moved back in, his relationship with his mother deteriorated. The next time I saw him, we went for a walk in his neighborhood to talk about the problem. I ended up suggesting that he would probably benefit from therapy, and he responded by commenting that a good friend could do the same thing as a therapist.

That left me groping for a reason why he should spend good money for psychotherapy when the equivalent, in his mind, could be acquired at no cost.

I ended up responding that there were no easy substitutes for the objectivity that a therapist brings to a problem and the training therapists undergo to help people find solutions.

We construct our own reality. Each of us has created an elaborate world in which we live, with its own rules, beliefs, and premises. That world is so real to us that we fail to recognize it's a personal construction. Changing the way we view our circumstances can free us of many of our relationship difficulties.

Psychotherapists Bruce Ecker and Laurel Hulley provide a clever illustration of how we construct reality. They pose the following dilemma. Imagine a live goose inside a bottle with a narrow neck. How does one get the goose out of the bottle without harming the goose or breaking the bottle?

Take a moment to think about it.

The answer is surprisingly simple. Poof! The goose is out!

The goose doesn't exist in the physical world, nor does the bottle. They exist only in our heads, so the rules of the physical world don't apply. In the mental world of imagination, it is easy to get the goose out of the bottle. But if one operates under the assumption that the goose and bottle are real, there is no answer to the dilemma.

Our problems with difficult people can be like the goose in the bottle. They seem so real that we don't recognize how much they are a product of our own perceptions and beliefs. When someone says that your problems are "all in your head," it may be a cliché, but it's a cliché with more than a grain of truth.

Therapy is a process of uncovering the beliefs and perceptions and emotional wounds at the root of our difficulties. To continue the answer I gave my friend on that walk, while a perceptive friend might be able to help us do this, a therapist is trained in how to do it and has a systematic strategy.

If you have never been in therapy and are contemplating the process, I'd like to offer a few suggestions that may prove helpful in selecting someone with whom to work.

• Ask for recommendations. A health professional or mental-health association is a good starting point; consider asking trusted friends as well. Often the very best therapists don't advertise and have few openings in their schedule. There are variations in therapists just as in any profession; some are better than others.

• See at least two different therapists before you make a decision. If your insurance requires that you go to a specific clinic, try to interview the available therapists over the phone before picking one. Ask if there is a fee for a phone conversation.

• Consider working with someone your own age or older. We all go through predictable life stages, and it is helpful if your therapist is going through or has gone through your stage, rather than merely having studied it in graduate school. Also, there is no substitute for life experience to develop wisdom. The best therapists are often those who have undergone crises and successfully transformed their own lives.

• Come to the first session with questions and a clear description of your problem. Has the therapist treated your problem before? Successfully? What is his or her training? Treatment orientation? Philosophy toward medication? How long might the therapy take? What are the financial policies? Policies for a missed visit?

• The therapist should have training and credentials from a recognized and accredited program that offers an academic degree, regardless of the approach to treatment. The type of degree and type of training are less important than the relationship that develops between the two of you.

• Be wary of people who possess special psychic or healing gifts or have learned a recently developed technique at a series of workshops. The problem is not with the gifts or skills, because these can be helpful and valid. The problem is in the way they are used. Regardless of the skill or technique being used, a therapist needs to have training in the basic principles of helping another in a therapeutic setting. Therapists without training may unconsciously view your progress in therapy as a validation of their talent or ability to heal, which distorts the process and robs you of the best treatment.

• If you see a therapist who specializes in your problem, be careful that you are not viewed merely as a diagnostic category rather than as a multifaceted person who happens to have a particular problem.

• Rapport is the most critical element in success. You want to feel that your therapist treats you with the utmost respect and empathizes with your pain. Your interactions should feel as if you are talking to a real person. The relationship between the two of you should feel warm and open.

• If you have a spiritual orientation to life, or if your religion is important to you, be sure that the therapist you choose is respectful of your beliefs. But don't choose someone specifically because he or she shares your beliefs. That doesn't necessarily make for a good therapist, and it might shut out other points of view that could help you.

• Try to find a therapist who incorporates forgiveness into therapy. There are therapists who will help you with your feelings about a difficult person, but not all are oriented toward forgiving the hurt.

• You will get the best results if you are genuinely willing to look at yourself and learn, however uncomfortable your discoveries might be. If you are there just to feel better by paying someone to listen, that's all you will get from the process.

• Once a solid and comfortable relationship has been established, if something happens to you in therapy that evokes a strong emotional reaction, you have hit pay dirt. Discomfort is telling you something important. Pay close attention. But if you continue to feel discouraged in the course of your therapy, and don't see progress, it is important to examine why. It could be that you have some especially difficult issues to resolve, or you might just need to work with a different therapist.

• Ultimately, what you learn about yourself has to be accepted by *you*. If you and your therapist have hit upon a personal truth, it will either feel right or it will feel uncomfortable—you won't have a neutral reaction. Don't accept an observation or diagnosis just because you paid money for it, or because the therapist has an advanced degree and you don't.

Therapy is a process of learning about yourself.

Group Therapy

> *The meeting of two personalities is like the contact of two chemical substances; if there is any reaction, both are transformed.*
>
> C. G. Jung

Sometimes our difficulties with others result in part from our own underdeveloped relationship skills. As painful as it may be to admit, there are times we contribute to our own difficulties through ineffectual ways of communicating. Yes, we can be difficult, too.

One cannot develop relationship skills alone. By definition, a relationship requires another person. Group therapy provides a safe opportunity to work on interpersonal skills. If you've ever asked the question, "Why do people treat me this way?" group therapy can help. It can offer a variety of helpful, transforming experiences:

- By sharing your concerns with the group, you discover you are not alone; others have similar problems.
- Group members will give you feedback to let you know if your perceptions of a situation are accurate or distorted.
- Group members will give you feedback about the way others see you, which may not be the way you see yourself.
- You have an opportunity to practice being honest and open with your feelings, something few of us do well.
- Others in the group can offer helpful suggestions and advice about your problem.
- Hope arises from the realization that others have experienced problems similar to yours and have solved them.
- By watching others in the group, you learn new relationship skills.
- By listening to others in the group, you gain new insights.

- Others in the group may remind you of people in your family of origin and help you to get in touch with and resolve old hurts.

Group psychotherapy can help if you want to improve your interpersonal skills.

Looking to Dreams for Guidance

The dream is the small hidden door in the deepest and most intimate sanctum of the soul.

C. G. JUNG

Most of the time, our attention is directed externally. We tend to focus much more on our outer circumstances than we do on what is happening inside us. When we are grappling with a difficult person, our tendency is to focus on what they are doing to us rather than looking within and examining our own thoughts and feelings.

Dreams are an ancient and universal method of accessing inner reality to discover what we are really thinking and feeling. Dreams can offer us a new way of seeing and understanding our difficulties in relationships and have the potential to bring about powerful breakthroughs.

Our inner self is elusive. It is abstract, intangible, and enigmatic. Dreams are a powerful way to contact the inner self because they have these same qualities.

Dream analysis has three components: first, the desire to remember one's dreams; second, a conscious intention to experience a dream with images and content that will solve a specific problem; and third, a framework for interpreting the resulting dreams. Here are some helpful starting points:

- Make a commitment to pay attention to your dreams on a daily basis. Buy a blank notebook or bound book to record them.

- Keep your dream journal, pen, and a flashlight or dim lamp next to your bed.
- Avoid alcohol consumption before going to sleep. It inhibits dream recall.
- Before going to sleep, focus on the desire to remember your dreams when you arise.
- Before you fall asleep, lie relaxed in bed and direct your mind toward the clear intention that your dreams will reveal information about your relationship difficulties with a specific person. Repeat your intention several times.
- If you wake up in the middle of the night, gently sit up and write down a few key images or phrases to facilitate fuller recall in the morning.
- Upon awakening, lie quietly before opening your eyes and review your most recent dream. Recall is sometimes helped by reviewing the dream in reverse order, starting with the images you remember just as you awaken. Before you get out of bed, write down as much of the story as you can remember, but write it in the order in which it happened. Write in the present tense, as if the dream is happening now, and give each dream a title. Include your initial interpretation, events of the previous day, how you felt during and after the dream, key characters, and anything else that may be relevant.
- The main question to always ask yourself when interpreting any dream is: "What comes to my mind as I consider this dream?" Dream interpretation relies on association. If, for example, the color blue is prominent in your dream, what does blue mean to you? It could represent the sky, the ocean, a color someone wore yesterday, or your mood. Don't try to overanalyze your dream images, however, or you will lose the important sense of wonder.
- Share your dreams with a therapist, dream partner, or group to help you remember and interpret them. But recognize that

ultimately you are the only one who can interpret the meaning of your dreams for yourself; others can only offer opinions. You will know when you have come up with a meaningful interpretation because it will be accompanied by a subtle sense of inner knowing, a shift inside you that has an "aha" or "I get it" feeling.

• Be attentive to recurring themes, characters, or images; these can represent your deepest life values and purpose. Be open to different interpretations of your dreams. Periodically review previous dreams. You might even want to create an index of dream images in your dream journal.

• Characters in dreams can represent you or someone else. Start by viewing everything in each dream as if it were an aspect of yourself, especially when a dream includes the difficult person with whom you are grappling. In other words, become the figures in your dreams. Each image and character can tell you about hidden aspects of yourself. Ask yourself, What does the figure want or need? What is the gift of this character's perspective? Once you have done this, consider what the dream might mean if it were about someone else.

• Have conversations with the characters in your dreams. Ask them who they are, what they want, what they represent, and why they acted the way they did. You will find that surprisingly helpful answers come from these unusual queries.

• If positive, compelling, attractive images come in your dreams, try to bring the same qualities into your outer life. If, for example, you dream of rainbows, buy a picture of a rainbow and put it somewhere in your environment.

By analyzing your dreams, you can gain insight into your difficult relationships. Dreams have been used in many cultures for thousands of years to acquire a deeper understanding of life's problems.

Meditation

The root of everything is meditation. It is a very great and lofty concept, making a person worthy of all holiness.

RABBI CHAIM YOSEF DAVID AZZULAI

There are many techniques of meditation and many philosophies about what it is. It can be done sitting or standing, eyes open or closed, with religious intention or strictly for health benefits. Nevertheless, there are common features to most practices.

First, meditation involves the cultivation of silence. Our minds are usually filled with mental clutter; meditation is a way to quiet the mind. Over time, silence comes to be maintained in activity, and we feel more calmness in daily life.

Second, meditation helps us to pay attention. The mind has a tendency to wander and become inattentive; meditation teaches us to pay attention by providing an intentional point of focus.

Third, meditation puts us in touch with our bodies, emotions, and thought patterns. By turning our attention inward instead of outward, we become more and more in tune with what is happening inside.

Fourth, meditation helps us to experience the divinity within. The Holy One is not out there somewhere in an abstract heaven; holiness resides in every human heart.

Meditation has been practiced for thousands of years in a spiritual context in virtually all religious traditions. In recent years, it has been demystified and endorsed as having a variety of medical benefits. But if we practice meditation solely for practical reasons, much of its majesty is lost to us.

Meditating to deal with difficult people has both practical and spiritual advantages. On a practical level, meditation can help to moderate our emotional reactivity to a difficult person. By becoming calmer, we are able to respond more appropriately to someone who bothers us. In addition, meditating allows us to become more attuned to the ways in which our body responds to a difficult person; this provides us with useful information about the situation.

Spiritually, meditation can bring answers to the interpersonal dilemmas we face. By stilling our mind, we are able to hear the quiet, delicate, intuitive impulses that provide guidance and direction in our life. Meditation allows us to get in touch with something greater and vaster than our problem, putting it in perspective. Experiencing infinity makes any problem less urgent and helps us to recognize that all of life's experiences have a purpose.

Meditation is one of the most ancient and holy ways to heal.

Praying for Guidance

I have been driven many times to my knees by the overwhelming conviction that I had nowhere else to go.

ABRAHAM LINCOLN

During a visit to Jerusalem, I heard a story from a rabbi about a nonbeliever who had become religious after an auto accident. His car sailed off the side of the road and was demolished, but miraculously he was unhurt. He felt that the circumstances were so extraordinary that his life must have been saved by God's intervention, so from that point on he took upon himself the many obligations of an observant Jew.

The rabbi described his response when the nonbeliever first approached the rabbi to learn. "So," said the rabbi, "you think God is like Superman? You think God rescues people when they get into trouble? What you don't realize is that God both sent you off the cliff *and* rescued you. God was trying to get your attention."

The fascinating, unsolvable dilemma of spiritual life is that

God is both the problem and the solution. God sends us our difficulties and God heals them. Why? To get our attention.

Difficulties come our way because we have become lost in the compelling complexities of outer life. One of the reasons for any type of suffering is to help us find our way back home, to recover the inner spiritual self that we have forgotten.

Prayer is a holy link to that spiritual self. Prayers are always answered when offered with sincerity, although the answer may take a different form than we expected or desired. We may not get what we pray for, but we always get what we need.

There are several obstacles to prayer. The first is that many of us never learned how to really pray—we just learned how to recite words from a book. The second is that we may find it uncomfortable to talk to someone who doesn't appear to be there. And a third obstacle arises from the negative associations picked up early in life in church or synagogue.

The most obvious prayer for those who are dealing with a painfully difficult relationship would seem to be, "Please make this go away." But when we ask for our tribulations to be lifted, we are essentially saying to God, "I'm not interested in learning this lesson." The Universe has presented us with a gift (admittedly in packaging we may not care for), yet we spurn it.

Perhaps praying instead for insight, guidance, and patience is more in keeping with a spirit of appreciation and a desire for learning and growth.

Answers to prayers can come through inner understanding, other people, or chance messages from the environment. Be open and receptive to what might come.

In the process of writing my doctoral dissertation, I had an unpleasant falling out with my graduate advisor. At one stage, after four revisions, he deliberately delayed reading my thesis for a period of seven months, as my frustration, anxiety, and anger mounted. Out of desperation, I prayed.

Nine days later, I was driving to my office in Minneapolis on Interstate 94. In a sudden rush just as I was crossing the Mississippi River from Saint Paul, I began to have a series of lucid insights into the nature of our difficulties and the way to resolve them. I clearly felt my prayers had been answered. Why it took nine days and why it happened on an expressway at fifty-five miles per hour is still a mystery to me.

A chance encounter at a restaurant, an unexpected phone call from a friend, a book randomly chosen from a bookstore, a segment overheard on the radio—all are among the possible avenues through which answers to prayers might come.

Some suggestions for writing your own prayers are presented in the Explorations section of this chapter.

To pray, just ask from the heart. No previous experience is necessary.

Blessings

Bless them that curse you, do good to them that hate you, pray for them which despitefully use you, and persecute you.

MATTHEW 5:44

When Cindy moved from a small town in the Midwest to New York City for graduate school, she was not prepared for the beggars, panhandlers, and homeless people that she encountered. They made her very uncomfortable, and she found herself in a quandary. She felt bad not giving them money, but she also felt bad giving money that she knew frequently went to buy alcohol or support a drug habit.

A friend suggested that when accosted she offer a silent blessing. This was a concept that was new to her. In this way, she could always give something precious.

So each time she encountered someone looking for a hand-out, she would offer them the following silent blessing: "May God bless you and heal your pain."

If prayer involves asking God to transform our own suffering, then to bless another is to move into partnership with the divine to help transform that person's suffering.

When a blessing is given, divine energy is invoked. The beauty of the process is that in order to give a blessing to another, the person who is giving the blessing is brought into a blessed state.

Our discussion of karma and divine justice in chapter 4 is relevant here. If hurtful actions can come back to the doer in a negative fashion, then blessed actions may similarly bless the doer in a positive fashion. This is why it is unwise to curse another.

Practically speaking, how can blessing be used to heal our difficulties? First, we can ask for blessings from others to give us the strength to deal with our trials. Second, we can bless the person with whom we are having difficulties.

Asking for a blessing from friends and family is a wonderful way to ask for both human and divine help and gives those who care about us a tangible way to express their wish to help us.

Blessing someone who has harmed us is a trickier issue. When someone has hurt us, doing something positive can be the last thing we consider. Often, our thoughts turn toward getting even. But if giving a blessing is the opposite of plotting revenge, then by giving a blessing we are invoking healing instead of causing harm. When we bless our adversary, we are helping ourselves.

How might we go about blessing a person who has caused us hurt? Perhaps we can take a clue from the musical *Fiddler on the Roof*. When the rabbi is challenged to come up with a prayer for the czar, the bane of existence for Jews in prerevolutionary Russia, he exclaims: "May God bless and keep the czar . . . far away from us!"

If we are still in a state of emotional pain, it is not easy to think about, much less offer something positive to, the one who has hurt us. But the potential is there for deep healing if we can.

A blessing is something positive we can give without involving the other person. It is something positive we can do that could improve the situation. And it is something positive we can offer that will come back to us favorably.

The Explorations section of this chapter offers suggestions for receiving blessings from friends and family and for blessing a foe.

Blessings transform suffering into holiness.

Affirming Your Desire for Healing and Forgiveness

A wise man will make haste to forgive, because he knows the true value of time, and will not suffer it to pass away in unnecessary pain.

SAMUEL JOHNSON

When Anne's company, based in Milwaukee, offered her a desirable promotion and transfer that required her to relocate to Baltimore, it was a tough decision for her. She had just started dating Larry four months earlier, and for two people in their early thirties looking to get married, the relationship appeared too promising to abandon. But the promotion represented everything Anne had worked for and wanted since college. Finally, after a week of reflection and conversation with Larry, she accepted the offer. They would attempt to continue the relationship long-distance.

Anne moved. She loved the new job and new city but missed Larry. At first they saw each other almost every weekend, but slowly the visits grew less frequent, and Larry grew more distant emotionally. Several months after the move, Larry confessed to Anne that he had begun an affair with a married woman at work.

Anne was crushed by the way he ended their relationship. The hurt was deep and lingered in her heart. The only time it was out of her mind was when she was too busy at work to think about it. Evenings were the worst.

Out of desperation one night, when she felt especially dejected, she spontaneously began to talk out loud to Larry's picture, expressing her anguish, disappointment, and desire to get past the sense of betrayal. She found it a powerful way to let out her painful feelings, so she continued the experiment. After several weeks, she began to feel easier, and the intensity of her grief subsided. At that point, she realized that it was important for her to forgive Larry and let go. She began to express her feelings of forgiveness to the picture. Each time, she felt a sense of release.

Without realizing it, Anne was practicing forgiveness affirmations. An affirmation is a technique for clarifying and expressing one's desires. Earlier in this chapter, we pointed out how important it is to have a clear desire to heal, and we discussed the value of speech for expressing emotion. Anne combined the two, accelerating the process of working through her intense feelings.

Once she felt the desire to forgive, Anne's process moved from the emotional to the spiritual.

The Explorations section at the end of this chapter offers some suggestions for using forgiveness affirmations to heal your difficulties.

By affirming what we want from a relationship, we move in the direction of getting it. By forgiving, we heal our own pain.

Inner Work and Outer Play

I've taken my fun where I've found it.

RUDYARD KIPLING

HEALING THE DIFFICULTIES

This chapter has focused on inner strategies for healing. Inner work, as the foundation for healing relationship difficulties, is all too often neglected.

Still, too much attention to inner work can make one preoccupied and self-absorbed. Outside activity is necessary as a balance. Here are some simple observations about activities that can also help you in the healing process:

- Find activities that bring you joy; you've experienced enough pain. Think of things you can do alone or with others that bring you delight and warm your heart.
- Get silly and have fun. Relationship difficulties can become much too serious.
- Let your friends know that you are having a hard time, and ask for their support.
- Spend time doing things that help you to think about something or someone other than yourself. Help a friend or do volunteer work. Serving others is wonderfully therapeutic.
- Consider attending lectures and taking classes that enhance your learning.
- If your lifestyle is sedentary, start doing something that requires physical activity.
- Pay attention to what you eat; be sure you are getting adequate nutrition and are not using food for emotional nourishment.
- Do something completely new and different that you've never done before.
- Find ways to express your spiritual longings and deepen your spiritual experience.

Even though doing inner work is critical for healing relationship difficulties, it needs to be balanced with healthy activity.

Explorations

WHEN SOMEONE IS A PAIN

Purpose: To overcome resistance to healing by understanding the advantages and disadvantages of holding on to negative feelings about a difficult person

Pick the person who is bothering you the most, the one about whom you have the most negative feelings. On a sheet of paper, make two columns with the following headings: Advantages and Disadvantages.

Start by listing the advantages of having these feelings. Be brutally honest with yourself—no one will see this except you. What do you get by having these bad feelings?

For example, you might get sympathy from friends whenever you complain to them about this person. Or you might feel superior to the person because *you* would never do such a terrible thing to someone else.

When your Advantages list is done, turn to the Disadvantages list. The question here is not about what the person is doing to you, but about the feelings you are having. How are you being hurt by holding on to these negative feelings?

For example, you might have insomnia because you lie awake at night thinking about the problem. Or you feel guilt because your desire for revenge isn't in keeping with your ethical values.

Now ask yourself if you still want to hold on to your negative feelings. Do the advantages outweigh the disadvantages? If they do, consider whether there are other ways to get the same benefits. For example, can you get sympathy from others without having an interpersonal disaster in your life? Can you feel good about yourself without having to feel superior to someone else?

WHAT HAVE YOU LOST?

Purpose: To identify the losses you have experienced in your dealings with a difficult person, and their implications

Step 1	Focus on a particular difficult person. See if you can identify what you've lost as a result of your encounters with the person. Here are some possibilities:

	Material	Money, shelter, possessions, health, mobility, physical safety.
	Nonmaterial	Freedom, pride, safety, control, comfort, dignity, love, belonging, trust, peace of mind, self-confidence, dreams for the future, belief that the world is fair.

Step 2	Revenge is one way that people try to even the score and get compensation for their losses. Your revenge fantasies can tell you a lot about what has been taken from you. What you fantasize about doing to someone else will give you further clues about your own losses. Just remember, it's okay to fantasize a bit, but don't act on your thoughts of revenge.
Step 3	Pay attention to what you are feeling as you identify your losses. Don't try to push the feelings too far away or distract yourself from them. Close your eyes if it helps you to stay with the feelings. They will gradually subside if you allow them into your awareness.

Step 4	Now, make a list of exactly what the difficult person has taken from you. For example, you list might say: By criticizing me at work in front of coworkers, my boss has taken away my self-respect and feeling of safety at work. You might want to read the list out loud (privately), so the reality of your losses is even more concrete.
Step 5	Have you had these feelings before at an earlier time in your life? Are the feelings familiar? If they are, these are your areas of vulnerability, the places inside that need healing.
Step 6	Congratulate yourself for your honesty. It is not easy to admit what has been lost and may never be recovered.

RIDING YOUR FEELINGS

Purpose: To develop the ability to stay with intense feelings as a way to heal them

The next time you experience intense feelings, try to stay with them for a while. Allow them to be in your awareness. Accept their presence. Don't push them down. Don't distract yourself from them. Don't try to figure them out. In other words, don't do anything except *feel* them.

Try not to talk or do anything until they subside. If someone else is present, just tell the person that you are fine and need a few moments to be with yourself. While it is always helpful to get support from others when you are emotionally distraught, the idea here is for you to experience your feelings so that you can allow them to be healed. No matter how intense, most of the time your feelings will subside naturally.

If it's helpful, recall an image of a bucking bronco. You are trying to stay on the horse. Remind yourself that your feelings can't hurt you; you are safe as long as you are on the horse.

You will probably "fall off the horse" lots of times in the beginning. If you can, try to get back on—allow yourself to reexperience your feelings if you have tried to push them down or distract yourself.

Don't force yourself to stay with your feelings if it becomes too uncomfortable. The trick is to find the right relationship with your feelings. You don't want to ignore or suppress them, but at the same time you don't want to be overwhelmed by them. If they become too intense, use imagery to put them at a distance. Imagine them across the street or in another state. In this way you can still feel them, but they aren't overpowering.

Another thing you might want to try is closing your eyes. Let your attention center on your body. If your attention is drawn to an uncomfortable physical sensation, that's a good sign—by allowing your attention to be with that sensation, you permit the feelings to subside more quickly. This sensation could be at the site of the original emotional wound.

Don't forget to breathe! Breathing into the discomfort will help to release it.

Eventually, through practice, you will find that you can stay with your feelings more and more. You will become accustomed to the notion that nothing bad happens when you allow yourself to feel your emotional pain. You will know that the feelings will subside and be released after a while, and over time their intensity will gradually diminish.

Above all, you will come to realize that you are not your feelings, you are just having them.

Cautionary Note: If you are too uncomfortable doing this exercise and find that your feelings are too much to handle, you may want to seek professional help.

DEVELOPING BODY AWARENESS

Purpose: To increase your awareness of the bodily sensations associated with different emotional states and different people

This exercise is to be done sitting in a chair with your eyes closed. In order to do it properly, you will need to either have a friend read the following instructions to you or record them on a cassette and play it back. The "eyes closed" component is essential.

Sit comfortably and close your eyes. [5–10-second pause] Pay attention to your breathing. Observe how your abdomen rises and falls . . . notice the air moving through your mouth and nose. Don't try to change your breathing, just observe it. [15-second pause] Feel the chair that you're sitting in . . . notice how your back feels against the back of the chair, notice how your feet feel on the floor. Get inside your body. This is where you live, twenty-four hours a day. [15-second pause]

Now bring to your mind someone who loves you very much. It could be a spouse, a child, a parent, a grandparent, a lover. Someone in whose presence you feel deeply loved. Just let that person come into your awareness. [15-second pause] Notice what happens in your body as you think about this person. Do you notice anything? Do you feel lightness in your heart, or a feeling of expansion in your head? A warmth in your stomach? Where in your body do you feel something shift, something different when you think about this person? [15-second pause] Give a name to your experience. How would you describe it to someone? [10-second pause]

Now say good-bye to this person who loves you and whom you love. Gently let the image leave your awareness. Sit quietly. [15-second pause]

Now bring to your mind someone with whom you are having difficulties. This time it won't be as pleasant. Try to be with whatever you're feeling. It can't hurt you, even though it may not feel good right now. [15-second pause] What are you feeling in your body this time when you think about the difficult person? Are you feeling a heaviness in your shoulders? A tightness in your chest? A queasiness in your stomach? Does your breathing change?

What are you noticing? [10-second pause] Give a name to this experience as well. How would you describe it to someone? [10-second pause]

Now you can let this person leave your awareness. Say good-bye and just sit quietly. Take a few deep breaths and breathe out the stress you have just experienced. [10-second pause] Open your eyes whenever you're ready.

Most people experience a distinct contrast in their reactions to the loving person and the difficult person. Our bodies respond this way all the time to all kinds of people, but we are rarely in touch with these subtle cues. Try to pay more attention to the signals that your body sends you as you interact with various people in your daily life. Use the information to supplement what your eyes and ears and mind are telling you.

If you didn't have physical sensations for either of the people or for both, this is useful information. You have shut down to protect yourself. Doing this shields you from further pain, but it also inhibits your capacity to experience joy and happiness.

Now that you've become familiar with the somatic contrast between loving people and difficult people, use this information as a tool to help you in your future dealings with difficult people. The next time someone upsets you, bring a loving person into your thoughts to counteract the unpleasant feelings that you are having.

A DIARY OF DEALINGS WITH A DIFFICULT PERSON

Purpose: To express your feelings and track your progress in healing a difficult relationship

Journal writing has a long tradition. This particular type of journal serves several purposes. First, it offers a way to acquire self-insight. As you write, you will learn new things about yourself.

Second, it will enable you to express your feelings about a difficult person as things happen without interruptions or backlash. You can be distraught, honest, funny, or nasty without worrying about anyone's reaction.

Third, it will show you your progress. The difficult person may not change, but you will, and your journal can provide a record of that change. When you're feeling down, you can review the journal and see where you once were.

Fourth, it will serve as a chronicle of the difficulties. If legal action ever becomes necessary, you will have a record of how you were mistreated. Such a record is essential if your problems are at work and you engage in litigation against your employer.

Have a separate notebook or bound book for your journal. If you use word processing, have a separate disk. Write as often as you wish for as long as you need to. You might want to write something every time you have contact with the difficult person, or every week, or whenever the mood strikes you.

You can write to an imaginary diary reader or to yourself, but try to avoid writing to the difficult person, because you are doing this for yourself, not for your adversary. Let your thoughts flow without censorship or editing.

Keep the journal private, don't do it on a computer at work, and don't mention its existence too readily. If you use word processing, see if you can lock the file with a password. I have heard too many unpleasant stories about private journals becoming public; I feel an obligation to provide a cautionary note.

THREE HEALING LETTERS

Purpose: To use writing as an outlet for emotional release

If your emotional energy is locked in your body, writing a letter to the person who is causing you pain is one way to express it.

These writing exercises are very simple and very powerful. But if you decide to do them, it is important to agree from the start that you will *not* be giving the letters you write to the person for whom they are intended. The purpose of this exercise is solely to allow you to release your emotions. It is not designed as a communication with the difficult person. That can also be done with a letter, but a different one.

If your letters are well written and it feels good to get your emotions out, you will be tempted to mail them. Resist the temptation! We will discuss how to best communicate with a difficult person in writing in the next chapter.

Letter 1:

Write a letter to the difficult person. Say whatever is on your mind. Don't hold back in language or tone. How were you hurt? What was taken away from you? How has your life been affected? How has your future been affected? What do you think of the person?

If you use word-processing software, it will be easy to make changes and additions as you think of new things to say. Take as much time as you need, and write the letter over several days or weeks if you find that your painful feelings continue to surface. Make the letter as long as you want.

As you write, pay attention to what is going on in your body. Your emotions are being released, and you may notice bodily sensations. Just keep writing.

Try reading the letter out loud with as much feeling as you can express. Imagine the difficult person is sitting in a chair in front of you, unable to respond, forced to listen to every single word without interruptions or defenses.

When you no longer experience intense feelings as you write or read the letter out loud, the letter is finished. Remember, don't mail it!

Cautionary Note: Once, after getting dumped by a girlfriend in college, I spent a week writing a letter like this. It felt great, and the letter said all the nasty things I wouldn't have been able to say to her face, so I mailed it. Ten years went by before we saw each other again.

Letter 2:

Now write the fantasy reply you would like to receive to letter 1. Write it as if you were the difficult person. What do you want to hear? What would you like the person to say to you that would ease your pain and make you feel better? What do you want to have acknowledged? How would you like the person to apologize and make amends?

Again, pay attention to what is happening to your feelings and to your body as you write.

You will probably never receive a letter like this, but it will feel good to express your wishes. You may also feel sadness at being hurt and not getting your needs met. Stay with your sadness; feeling it will help your healing.

Letter 3:

Write the difficult person a thank-you letter. Thank him or her for all the beneficial things he or she may have done for you. The pain of someone's difficult behaviors often overshadows any positive memories from your shared past. For example, you may currently be mad at your mother for the way she treats your spouse, but for years and years she may have done many things for you without receiving much appreciation or recognition.

Thank the person for helping you to learn your spiritual lessons, for teaching you patience and compassion, for making you more sensitive to the suffering of others, for helping you to develop skills that were dormant. Use chapter 4 to help give shape to what you've learned and to assess how you've changed for the better as a result of the difficulties.

If you can't come up with any thank-yous or anything positive to say, then your anger hasn't yet been vented, and you need to spend more time on letters 1 and 2.

COMPOSING YOUR OWN PRAYER

Purpose: To compose a specific prayer that will help to heal your relationship difficulties

Each spiritual tradition has its own prayers. Some are beautifully written and have been used by millions for centuries.

But there is a predicament to using a prayer composed by someone else, no matter how hallowed; it may not inspire. If you are not inspired by a prayer, then the most important element, intention, is missing. Empty words recited in a mechanical fashion invariably bring minimal results. That's why it's helpful to compose your own prayer.

When you first compose your own prayer, "Help" is a perfectly adequate starting point. When your car is stranded on the highway, a help sign will eventually bring you the assistance you need; it is not necessary to describe the difficulties in detail. In similar fashion, if the Universe can select our circumstances to provide us with the growth we need, then it undoubtedly also knows what we need in order to heal.

Most of us are inclined to say something more specific than "Help." Composing a written prayer will help you to focus, will promote reflection, and will get you into a regular habit.

When praying for insight and guidance, consider including the following elements in your prayer:

• Decide where to direct your prayers. I suggest that you always address the highest place/Being/concept that you can imagine.

You may want to choose a specific title: God, Almighty Father, Jesus, Holy One, Great Spirit, Master of the Universe, Higher Power, or whatever feels most comfortable to you. Praying for specific help from, for example, an angel or your deceased grandmother may bring that help; praying to the Holy One will bring the specific help you need from a variety of sources beyond your awareness or comprehension.

• Include an "I don't understand, please show me/teach me" section. What do you want to learn? How would you like to change? What would you like to see more clearly that is currently elusive?

• What qualities of character are you are trying to cultivate? For example, you might want to ask for help in acting with integrity or in developing patience and compassion.

• Offer your flaws. Give whomever you are praying to your anger, sadness, or feelings of superiority—whatever it is that you wish to overcome.

• If there is any possibility of your experiencing harm or danger, ask for protection. If there is any possibility that you might cause harm, ask for help in developing restraint.

• Consider ending with a thank-you. Express gratitude for the opportunity that has been given to you.

Here's a sample:

Holy One, please hear my request. You are the source of all healing. Please help me to resolve the difficulties I am having with _____ *. Please help me to understand why, in Your infinite wisdom, You have sent* _____ *into my life. Please bestow on me the clarity to see how we might heal our differences. Help me to be more patient and kind toward* _____ *, especially during those times when I am most likely to act in hurtful ways. I offer to You my bitterness and my rage; please accept them. When thoughts of revenge arise within me, let them evaporate like mist in the sun. Let no harm befall me or anyone else. I thank You from the full-*

ness of my heart for giving me this opportunity to perfect my
character and grow closer to You.

If you prefer not to offer a personal prayer with specific requests, compose a prayer of praise and acceptance. Offer a general prayer to God and accept that whatever happens is what is best for your spiritual growth. Here's an example:

Almighty, You are blessed as the source of all help and healing.
In Your infinite wisdom, You know what is best for all. May it be
Your will to satisfy the needs of all of Your Creation with Your
abundant mercy. Shine Your holy light upon us. May peace and
harmony prevail on earth as in heaven.

Use these prayers as often as you need to or want to. It helps to be regular. You might want to type your prayer and put it in a visible place as a recurring reminder—next to your bed, on the refrigerator, in your cubicle at work, or in your wallet.

Feel the silence and the majesty as you pray. You might even notice the feeling in the room changing.

Revise the prayer as your self-insight expands or as the relationship changes.

ASKING FOR BLESSINGS FROM OTHERS

Purpose: To learn how to receive a blessing from friends and family for support in resolving your difficulties

Praying for help with our difficulties is one way to request spiritual assistance. Another is to ask someone to give you a blessing.

Anyone can give blessings. Here are some recommendations if you want to receive blessings or give them:

• The person who will be giving the blessing should listen carefully to find out what the person receiving the blessing needs. For example, someone might need the ability to withstand an insult without an intense reaction or might wish to work on regaining trust after having been betrayed.

• The person who will be giving the blessing should elevate the other's needs to a spiritual level. For example, the ability to withstand an insult could also be seen as the capacity to recognize that human judgments are limited in their understanding and all judgment ultimately comes from God.

• The person giving the blessing should remind herself that all blessings come from God; the person giving the blessing is just a channel for the divine.

• The person giving the blessing should attempt to feel an inner state of love and peace toward the person receiving the blessing.

• The person giving the blessing should, if comfortable, look deep into the recipient's eyes and soul when speaking the blessing.

• Blessings are best when they are short and simple.

• If it's comfortable, you might want to place your hands on or over the other person's head when offering the blessing.

Here are several samples:

May you be blessed with the constant knowledge that God is your only judge.

May God bless you with the wisdom to choose the correct course of action in all of your dealings with _____.

May God bless you with insight into the reasons for your difficulties.

BLESSING A DIFFICULT PERSON

Purpose: To consider how a silent blessing might be offered to someone who has harmed you

To silently bless a difficult person, just think of positive attributes and spiritual qualities that you hope that person may acquire. However strange it may seem, you will discover it is actually fun to come up with blessings for people who drive you crazy. One whimsical way to think about it is to remind yourself that whatever you wish for your worst enemy will also be given to you. Here are some examples. Feel free to substitute the terms Almighty, Jesus, Holy One, Great Spirit, Master of the Universe, Higher Power, or whatever appeals to you.

For someone who is oblivious to his or her effect on others:
Almighty, I ask that _____ be blessed with an appreciation of the pain s/he causes others.
For someone who is always putting others down:
Almighty, I ask that _____ be blessed with growing self-confidence and the recognition that it is not necessary to put others down to feel good.
For someone who has angry outbursts:
Almighty, I ask that _____ be blessed with calmness and self-control.
For someone who has cheated you:
Almighty, I ask that _____ be blessed with an appreciation of the workings of divine justice.
For someone who is arrogant:
Almighty, I ask that _____ be blessed with the quality of humility before becoming humbled.
For someone who is envious:
Almighty, I ask that _____ be blessed with a longing to know You instead of a longing for what others have.
For a tyrannical boss (inspired by *Fiddler on the Roof*):
Almighty, I ask that _____ be blessed with a wonderful new job that takes him/her to another company.

Using Affirmations to Heal the Difficulties

Purpose: To learn how to use forgiveness affirmations to heal relationship difficulties

Here are some suggestions for using forgiveness affirmations:
- It is helpful to have a focal point. A picture is ideal, but if you don't have one, write the person's name in the center of a blank piece of paper.
- Look at the picture or paper as you do the affirmations.
- Although it may seem awkward and silly, talk out loud to the picture or paper. Silent affirmations aren't as effective, because talking frees emotion.
- Express your pain. Tell the person via the picture or paper how much you were hurt and how bad you feel. Take your time, but try not to go on and on.
- Next, express what you want from the person or relationship. Do you want to be treated with respect? Do you want to recover a lost friendship? Do you want hassle-free interactions?
- If you can, express forgiveness. Tell the person via the picture or paper that you forgive them.
- Continue the exercise for as long as you continue to have strong feelings about the person.

Expect very intense feelings to arise from this exercise. Allow yourself to feel them as discussed earlier (see the exercise entitled "Riding Your Feelings" in this chapter). Put your attention into your body or breathe into your feelings if they are too strong. You will know the exercise is working if there is a reduction in the intensity of your feelings over time.

CHAPTER 6

EMBRACING THE ADVERSARY

A Biblical Tale of Reconciliation

Esau ran to meet him [Jacob], flung himself upon his neck, and kissed him. And they wept.

GENESIS 33:4

Earlier in this book, we discussed a biblical story from chapters 27 and 29 of Genesis in which Jacob, the son of Isaac, deceives his father, cheats his older brother Esau out of the family birthright, and flees. Jacob is later deceived himself in parallel fashion by his uncle Laban, illustrating how divine justice operates through human interaction. The continuation of this story in chapters 32 and 33 of Genesis is relevant to our current concern, the resolution of relationship difficulties face-to-face.

As the story unfolds, we read about how Jacob attempts to make contact with his estranged brother after twenty years have passed. Now married and wealthy, he sends messengers to Esau, instructing them to tell his brother that he seeks "to find favor in your eyes."

His messengers return to tell him that Esau is already on his way with four hundred men. Fearful and distressed, Jacob prays for protection and decides to send an elaborate gift of various types of livestock to Esau, hoping it will appease his brother's wrath.

That night, after assisting his family across a stream, Jacob, left alone, is visited by a man. They wrestle until sunrise, and Jacob's hip is injured, but the man is unable to prevail; at dawn he asks Jacob to let him go. Jacob, however, insists on a blessing from the man first; the man, a divine being, bestows on him a new name: Israel. But when Jacob asks for the being's name, the being evades by replying, "Now why do you ask after my name?"

Jacob names the site of the encounter Face of God and limps to his family. He then spots Esau. As the brothers finally come face-to-face, Jacob walks ahead of his family and bows low to the ground seven times until he is close to his brother. Esau runs to him, and they embrace and kiss. The two men weep.

Perhaps the most striking aspect of this narrative of reconciliation is Jacob's supernatural wrestling match. Each element of the story has symbolic meaning.

The encounter takes place at night, an appropriate metaphor for the way we experience our relationship difficulties. We are frequently "in the dark" about how to resolve them and what they mean.

The narrative initially describes Jacob's wrestling opponent as a man, but at dawn he is revealed to be a divine being. When we are in the throes of a conflict with another person, we think the problem is with the person, but it is really about our own spiritual journey and the lessons we need to learn. The divine nature of our difficulties is concealed until the struggle is over and a deeper understanding comes, just as dawn brings to light the true nature of Jacob's adversary.

Jacob's bodily encounter with a divine being prior to his reconciliation with Esau symbolizes the need to deal with difficulties in relationships physically and spiritually first, before a personal meeting. Bodywork, meditation, prayer, therapy, and dream analysis are some of the ancient and modern ways that can be used to heal feelings and find meaning.

The word "wrestle" in the original Hebrew can also be translated as "embrace." While Jacob struggles to prevail over the being, he is simultaneously experiencing a sort of holy intimacy. Our trials, however painful, are given to us out of love; they bring us closer to God. It is only in times of distress that we are willing to completely open our hearts to heaven. When we wrestle with a difficult person, it is as if we are being embraced by God, even though the embrace is not a pleasant one.

While Jacob attempts to influence the outcome of his upcoming meeting by offering material gifts to Esau, it is his experience with the divine being that finally prepares him and appears to take away his fear. The long-anticipated meeting with Esau turns out favorably. While outer efforts clearly contribute to the resolution of difficulties, it is the inner spiritual work that creates a favorable atmosphere for a full reconciliation. When Jacob bests the divine being, he masters his spiritual lesson and feels he will be successful with his brother because he has triumphed over himself.

Jacob is wounded by his encounter with the being. He is not the same afterward, just as we are not the same after an encounter with a difficult person. In this case, Jacob is left with a limp. There is no question that difficulties in relationships leave lasting wounds.

But in this story, as in life, there is a gain to offset the loss. Jacob is given a new name, Israel, which can be translated as God-Fighter, because he has "fought with God and men and prevailed." Jacob is transformed by his encounter during the night just as our encounters with difficult people transform us. We are no longer the same person; we have grown spiritually from the experience. Jacob's wound is the price for his blessing; the emotional toll of our difficulties is the price we pay for spiritual growth.

Finally, there remains a mysterious element to Jacob's encounter. He does not learn the name of his mystical adversary but is instead asked why he needs to know. In our own life, we seek answers that elude us. We may never know the reason for our difficulties. We only need to know that they have been sent to us by God for a divine purpose. They are, more than anything, tests of faith.

The biblical story of Jacob and Esau is the archetype of healing and reconciliation in relationships. It offers us a multitude of perspectives for understanding our difficult relationships.

It's Difficult to Talk About the Difficulties

At best, the renewal of broken relations is a nervous matter.
HENRY BROOKS ADAMS

The prospect of discussing our problems with a difficult person face-to-face generally makes us uncomfortable. Jacob evaded a conversation with his brother for twenty years. Avoiding the discussion altogether is a common way to deal with our discomfort, but as we discussed in chapter 2, this just perpetuates the problem.

A woman who had just recovered successfully from major surgery came to one of my workshops because she was disappointed in several friends. They had not given her the emotional support she wanted and needed before and after her traumatic operation. After an exercise in which she wrote a letter pouring out her feelings, she told the group that while it felt good to express her feelings, she could never say in person what she had written. But when I asked her why, she couldn't articulate a clear reason.

We often resist saying what's on our mind to people we are upset with, even though we carry strong feelings. If pressed for a reason, we might say that we don't want to hurt *their* feelings. But there's another, less obvious reason. We are actually more afraid of our own feelings than we are of their reaction to what we say. We resist talking about the problem because we are afraid of experiencing certain emotions that the conversation is likely to bring up, emotions that make us uncomfortable.

If we avoid a conversation with someone because of an anticipated reaction, it is really our own response that we dread. The possibility that what we say might cause someone to feel bad, cry, get angry, lash out, or dislike us is something we don't want to feel, so we choose to not talk at all.

> It is possible to say anything to anyone. The only thing that stops us is our own reluctance to experience certain emotions. The other person's reactions are not the biggest barrier; ours are.

The Need to Talk

I was angry with my friend;
I told my wrath, my wrath did end.
I was angry with my foe;
I told it not, my wrath did grow.

WILLIAM BLAKE

When we don't talk about our problem face-to-face with the other person, we encounter several consequences. As has already been mentioned earlier in this book, the most obvious is that the problem continues to fester and doesn't get better. We are also stuck with unpleasant feelings that don't go away easily. And our energy is entangled in frustration instead of being invested in productive directions.

Often, what people do in this type of situation is to talk about the problem, but not with the person causing it. I had a college roommate who talked to everybody except me—I would hear his complaints about dirty dishes and late-night television watching from other people but never from him. Telling others makes one feel better in the moment but does nothing to resolve the difficulties.

Speaking up has a number of advantages. The first is that you get to stand up for yourself and assert your importance, your feelings, and your need to be listened to. Stating your legitimate wishes helps you to feel better about yourself.

When you speak up, you provide the other person with important information that may have been lacking. He or she may not know how you've been affected until you say something. Once, while doing volunteer work for a nonprofit agency, I shared responsibility for an important project with someone who contributed little and had absolutely no idea how much of the work I was doing. I was deeply resentful but still had a variety of excuses for not saying anything. He never knew, so things never changed.

It is often the case that solutions to the difficulties only develop when both parties engage in a discussion to arrive at them. Neither side holds a monopoly on the truth, and when each person shares his or her perceptions, feelings, and goals, the potential for a new solution can emerge.

Whenever possible, talk face-to-face with the person who is causing the difficulties.

What Do You Want from the Other Person?

It is a fault to wish to be understood before we have made ourselves clear to ourselves.

S I M O N E   W E I L

Your chances of success in a conversation with a difficult person will be enhanced if you know what you want. While this may seem elementary, it is all too often the case that people enter into conversations without clear goals. Without always realizing it, we all bring four different types of goals into every conversation with a difficult person—material goals, relational goals, emotional goals, and procedural goals.

Material goals are the specific, tangible things we want. This is what most of the discussion tends to center on. Let's consider the example of a new neighbor who has a troublesome barking dog that is keeping us awake at night. When, after approaching the neighbor several times, we find he has no interest in doing anything about our complaint, our goal is quite obvious—to get the beast to stop barking. When we communicate with the neighbor, that's what the conversation will be about. Our goal is to see some specific change in the material world: in this case, a dog's behavior.

The second type of goal, which is not as obvious as the first, is relational and tends to get talked about less, if at all. We also have as a goal the desire to define the nature of our relationship with the other person. This might involve clarifying our rights, specifying emotional distance or closeness, or defining power. We might, for instance, be the type of person who in general wants to have a more cordial and respectful relationship with our neighbors, while this particular neighbor might be the type who wants to be left alone and has no desire to interact.

Our third type of goal, even less obvious than the first two, involves our emotions, especially our self-esteem. Our goal in this context is always to maintain a positive self-image and manage feelings of shame and pride. If our self-image is threatened, we attempt to defend ourselves against feeling humiliated, embarrassed, ignored, or excluded. In the case of the neighbor, we seek to overcome the discomfort of having our wishes disregarded by another; the fact that our complaint is seen as unimportant may trigger in us feelings of inadequacy or powerlessness that we actively attempt to minimize. Our goal is to avoid experiencing certain negative emotions while striving to experience positive ones.

Our final type of goal has to do with procedure and concerns the way our difficulties are resolved. We have goals concerning the way that we'd like to see things settled and the amount of time it will take. Some might prefer a direct face-to-face discussion. Others might engage in written communication. Some might bring in a third party, or take legal action, or call the police. Returning to our uncooperative neighbor, we might prefer to sit down and talk, while our neighbor's style of interaction requires someone with a uniform showing up at the door, or a summons to show up in court.

We can sometimes get fixated on one type of goal without realizing the others are operating behind the scenes. With the now-infamous neighbor, we may obsess about getting the dog to stop barking. What we may fail to realize is that we have other less apparent goals that are just as important. We are also seeking to define the relationship (a relational goal), eliminate feelings of being ignored (an emotional goal), and avoid legal action (a procedural goal).

When some of our goals are clear to us but others are not, then even if we achieve our stated goals, we won't be satisfied, and we won't understand why. This often happens when talking to a difficult person. The material goals stay at the forefront because they are the obvious ones, while the other three types of goals remain in the background or aren't recognized at all. Nevertheless, they are still operating, and if they are not achieved, we will feel incomplete.

An exercise for clarifying goals can be found in the Explorations section at the end of this chapter.

> **If you're not sure just what outcome you want from a conversation with a difficult person, then you probably aren't going to get it.**

Letting Go

*Often enough our faith beforehand in an uncertain result
is the only thing that makes the result come true.*

WILLIAM JAMES

The dilemma we face when we state our wishes to another person
is that there is no guarantee we will attain them. Asking for something enhances our chances of getting it, but it doesn't necessarily
mean we will.

Let's return to our Genesis story. When Jacob decides that he
wants to reconcile with Esau, he doesn't know how things will
turn out. However, when he learns that Esau is approaching with
four hundred men, he becomes frightened and does two things.
He prays, and he sends Esau elaborate gifts. Clearly, he wants to
influence the outcome of their meeting on both material and spiritual levels, but there is no way for him to know what Esau will do
when they meet, and the indications thus far aren't favorable.

In our own encounters with a difficult person, any attempt to
improve the situation through discussion will have an uncertain
outcome. We cannot know how the other person will respond to
our initiative. That means all we can do is prepare for the conversation, hope for the best, and let go of our attachment to a particular result, since we may not get it.

We can prepare in a number of ways. We can do the inner
healing work described in chapter 5. We can practice our interpersonal skills and study negotiation strategies. We can be clear in
our own mind about our goals. But ultimately, we still don't know
what will happen.

**When talking with a difficult person, we only have control over
what we do. We cannot control what the other person does, and
we can't control how things will turn out.**

And Now for Something Completely Different

He that will not apply new remedies must expect new evils.

FRANCIS BACON

Chances are you have been stuck with your difficulties for a while, and they're still going on. Consider doing something you've never done before. Be creative. If it does work, you will have made progress. If it doesn't, you'll feel different about yourself because you tried something new, and you will have learned something that will help you in the future.

Once you've spent some time working on your goals and determining what you want to accomplish from your conversation, here are some helpful questions to ask yourself:

- What are some other, creative ways of achieving my goals?
- How is the difficult person likely to respond to each one; how will he or she likely feel?
- How am I likely to respond to each option; how would each one make me feel?
- What will I do if the other person doesn't respond to my strategy in the way I expect or hope?

Being creative means catching the other person off guard without hurting, harming, or making things worse. For example, if you have been attempting to talk about the difficulties to a coworker without success, try sending her a fax as a way to get her attention. Or write a silly poem about the problem. If your elderly neighbor is surly and unpleasant, bring her some home-baked cookies and act as if she's been your friend all along. If your mother-in-law is on your back, give her a gift certificate for a massage, especially if she's never had one before.

Doing something unexpected can often lead to a breakthrough in resolving the difficulties.

Treat the Other Person with Respect

*Respect . . . another person, not because he is wrong or
even because he is right, but because he is human.*

JOHN COGLEY

Respect is something given to people who earn it. The idea of
treating a difficult person with respect might strike you as both
distasteful and foreign.

But if you want to take a spiritual approach to your difficulties, respecting your enemy is the only option. You may not like
the other person, you may be furious at what's been done to you,
and you may disagree strongly with the person's beliefs. Nevertheless, as a fellow human being, the difficult person has as much
of a right to be here as you do. Saint John of the Cross made the
point succinctly when he said that the people you despise "may be
pleasing to God for . . . reasons which you cannot discover."

On a practical level, respecting a difficult person also makes
sense. People have pride. No one wants to be viewed as stupid,
wrong, illogical, pretentious, immature, naive, uneducated, ignorant, shallow, or thoughtless. When we do not exhibit respect for
others, these are the messages they receive from us, whether we
send them consciously or unconsciously.

Consider also the observation that most of the time, difficult
people don't realize they're being difficult. They expect to be
treated with respect just as we do, because they don't really see
the implications of what they're doing.

Put yourself in their shoes. You have been behaving a certain
way toward someone because you think it's appropriate or justified. Or else, you have no idea what it is you're actually doing to
the other person. You certainly wouldn't label yourself as difficult, even though the other person might see you that way. And
when the person gets upset, you can't figure out what the fuss is

all about, and you certainly don't like being treated with coldness or contempt.

Treating someone with respect prevents the difficulties from escalating. No one can continue to harbor anger at someone who is treating them with consideration. Respect also elicits the deeper truths underlying the difficulties that suspicion and distrust conspire to keep hidden.

Respect does not mean that you necessarily agree with the other person, that you condone what she's done or that you pretend to like her when you don't. And respecting another does not require you to be treated with disrespect yourself. It simply means that, as a fellow human being, the other person deserves the same courtesy and consideration that you would expect in the same circumstances.

In the story of Jacob and Esau, Jacob, upon meeting Esau face-to-face for the first time in twenty years, bows to the ground not once but seven times in an ancient gesture of humility.

Showing respect for a difficult person is an important step toward healing and reconciliation.

Make Sense of the Other Person's Point of View

Seek first to understand, then to be understood.

STEPHEN COVEY

In chapter 3 we discussed various reasons why people might be difficult. Understanding their behavior can take away some of our anguish, but now that we are getting ready to talk to the person, our primary concern is to meet our goals, not just to feel better.

Difficult people may do things that make no sense to us or

anyone else, but as we've pointed out, the things they do make sense to them. In their world, the behaviors they engage in fulfill a certain need or protect them from experiencing certain feelings. If we want to meet our goals, we must climb inside their world and understand it. There is a simple, powerful technique for doing this: It's called listening.

But the type of listening we need to do when we're talking with a difficult person is not the type we're accustomed to. Typically, we listen halfheartedly, all the while daydreaming, thinking of what we want to say next, or making judgments about what the other person has just said. Other people talk more slowly than we can think, so we have the luxury of not giving them our full attention while making it look as if we are.

If we want to really understand the other person, we need to really listen. Listening attentively is how we tangibly express the intangible concept of respect. Here are some points to consider about attentive listening:

• You are much more likely to be listened to respectfully yourself if you have first demonstrated to the other person that you are interested in hearing the other point of view and have understood it. Listening is therefore a necessary prerequisite for achieving your own goals.

• As we've discussed, everyone wants to be treated with respect. Refrain from judging or evaluating what the other person is saying while you're listening. Monitor your body language.

• What people say is only a part of what is going on. There are always unspoken needs and feelings behind their words. Listening as a skill involves gently bringing out what the other person is not expressing verbally to get at the real truth.

• One way to demonstrate understanding is to repeat what you've just heard. Use phrases like, "Here's what I think you're telling me . . ." "So you mean to say that . . ." "Let me check to see if I understood correctly; you just said . . ." "I want to be sure I heard right; you just told me . . ."

• A more sophisticated way to demonstrate understanding is to express the next logical step. Use phrases like, "If that's what you think, does that mean . . ." "Are you implying that we should . . ." "If that's your position, it suggests . . ." "If you want to take that direction, wouldn't it lead to . . ." Be careful not to use this approach to change the subject or show that you're smarter than the person speaking.

• Still another approach that strongly indicates your understanding is to gently express what you think the other person is feeling. Use phrases like, "I'd be furious if that happened to me." "I imagine you must be feeling very sad about what happened." "I can't imagine what I'd feel if I were in your shoes." "I'll bet you felt terrific afterward." "It seems to me that you must have been desperate for help when that happened to you." Be careful not to put the other person in the position of expressing feelings he is not ready to express. Also, try not to convey the notion that he should be having certain feelings if he's not.

• Show interest in hearing more from the person. Use phrases like, "Tell me more . . ." "What was it like?" "I'm not sure I understand . . ." "And then what happened?"

• Show interest nonverbally. Your body reveals how sincere your interest is. Make eye contact, nod your head, say, "Uh-huh," or "Oh!" Sit forward. Don't fidget or look at your watch.

• You are not done listening until you truly experience the other person's point of view. You will know that has happened when you feel the element of truth it contains. This does not mean that you have been persuaded to agree with the other's position; it does mean that you now see the other person differently and acknowledge that her point of view has some validity. She has earned some measure of your respect, because what you once found incomprehensible is now beginning to be understood.

Before your own point of view can get a proper hearing, you need to demonstrate to the other person that you sincerely want to understand that person's feelings.

The Importance of Honesty

If people would dare to speak to one another unreservedly, there would be a good deal less sorrow in the world a hundred years hence.

SAMUEL BUTLER

If, as we pointed out, the main barrier to talking with a difficult person face-to-face is our reluctance to deal with our own feelings, then not knowing what to say probably runs a close second. Participants in my workshops invariably come wanting a script they can take home, memorize, and recite. If only they knew the right retort or comeback, if only they were able to think of just the right comment, the problem would get better.

Perhaps we have learned this approach from years of watching television, where articulate actors spout clever lines from precisely written scripts. Seeing difficult relationship problems get solved in thirty minutes with a few well-timed words may have convinced us that we should be able to do the same.

No book, workshop, or therapist can tell us what to say to resolve our difficulties. We all possess the ability to say the right thing at the right time without any help. We simply need to listen to the other person carefully and respectfully and then speak from our own heart with honesty and sincerity.

The inner work described in chapter 5 prepares us to do this.

Will served on the advisory board of a prominent community organization. After being on the committee for five years, he noticed that his name was not listed on the newly printed brochure for the current year, so he called the executive director to look into what he assumed was an oversight. She informed him that he had been removed from the committee a few months earlier and she hadn't yet gotten around to telling him.

He felt instant outrage, and after alternately being silent and sputtering into the phone, he told her that he didn't want to continue the conversation because he was afraid he would say something he'd later regret. Will ended up writing a carefully crafted letter to the executive director, expressing his upset at being treated so unprofessionally after putting in hundreds of hours of service. He knew why he'd been removed—he was not in favor of a major new initiative that the executive director was trying to get approved, and she was able to convince the advisory board chair to have him replaced. But there were more diplomatic and respectful ways to deal with someone like Will.

Several months passed, and Will thought he'd forgotten about the incident until he unexpectedly ran into the executive director while shopping. All Will's anger returned in that moment. He asked her if she could spare a few moments to talk. To her credit, she was willing, although understandably guarded. The two sat down in a nearby coffee shop.

He started the conversation by telling her that he was still angry about what had happened, didn't want to continue feeling that way, and wanted to reach some kind of closure. She proceeded to coldly recite her official position for fifteen minutes, repeating the same flaccid arguments that she had expressed in her reply to his letter, never once admitting to what they both knew had really happened. After getting nowhere, he paid the bill, got up to leave, and said, "You know, we used to have a nice working relationship, and I'm really sad that it's ending like this."

To his surprise and her embarrassment, she began to cry. After regaining her composure, she congratulated him on being the first person ever to see her cry over a work-related issue. He told her that had not been his intent.

Her professional facade had now evaporated, and the real person emerged. They had an honest talk that completely resolved his negative feelings. A few days later, he even received a thank-you note from her.

Looking back, what struck Will so vividly about this incident was that he didn't really know what he was doing. The discussion was unplanned, and he didn't have a strategy or an idea of what he wanted to say. Will was simply being spontaneous and honest about what he was feeling at that moment. Something about his honesty helped both of them to break through their defensive feelings.

To talk with a difficult person, you don't always have to know what to say. You just need to be honest about what you're feeling.

Put the Difficulties in Perspective

O Lord, that lends me life,
Lend me a heart replete with thankfulness!
WILLIAM SHAKESPEARE (*Henry VI, Part Two*)

Very few people act consistently difficult. In most cases, people trouble us only some of the time; at other times their effect on us is neutral or even positive. We have a history with each and every difficult person in our lives. Some histories are brief, while others go back to birth.

Our memory of these histories is frequently faulty. If someone does something that drives us crazy, we are consumed by the emotions of the moment and tend to forget other positive experiences we've had together. The very people we are most upset with may be the ones who have done the most for us in the past without receiving any recognition or gratitude. We tend to focus on the negative things people do to us without paying sufficient attention to the positive.

Gregg Krech, an organizational psychologist and teacher of Buddhism, tells the story of one of his students, a woman who had to work late and was unable to get to the company parking lot by the official 6:00 P.M. closing. Normally, the attendant would shut the gate and go home at that time. The woman arrived at 6:20 to find the gate was indeed locked. The attendant hadn't yet left; however, he refused to open the gate, citing policy. She finally found someone who ordered the attendant to release her car. Understandably, the woman was furious.

When she told her teacher about the incident, he encouraged her, much to her dismay, to buy the attendant a gift. There was no question the attendant had been uncooperative that evening, but he had also taken good care of her car for as long as she had been working there. She was fixated on the one incident while forgetting the ongoing service she had received, for which she had never given proper thanks.

How is this perspective on gratitude relevant to our concern about talking with a difficult person? Because we need to take the whole person and the entire history of the relationship into consideration when we meet. Having an awareness of the positive things that the person has done for us in the past will soften our heart. If we express our appreciation as a part of the conversation along with our grievance, it will also soften that person's heart toward us.

> **Preparation for a discussion with a difficult person includes a mental review of the positive things done for us in the past so that we don't focus exclusively on the negative. This is yet another way of showing respect.**

Don't Let the Other Person's Behavior Dictate Yours

The test of a man or woman's breeding is how they behave in a quarrel.

GEORGE BERNARD SHAW

A man took a stroll with a friend to a corner newsstand and bought a paper. The person at the newsstand was surly and unpleasant, but the man who bought the paper remained congenial and cordial. His surprised friend asked him why he was being so nice to someone who didn't seem to deserve it. The man replied, "Why should I let his behavior dictate mine?"

Some people consciously choose to be rude, annoying, aggressive, or abrasive because it works for them. It keeps people away, or it gets them what they want, and they don't seem to realize or care how alienating they are to others. But we have a choice regarding how we respond.

I vividly remember one incident early in my teaching career when a student came to my office complaining about an exam grade. I explained my grading system and how his grade had been assigned, but he wasn't satisfied. He continued to argue with me, restating the same unconvincing argument over and over in a louder and louder voice, clearly expecting I'd give up and give in. Instead, I looked at him calmly and said, "I'll bet that works really well when you use it on your parents. But if you want to get me to change my mind, you're going to have to try something else, because it's not working right now." Startled by my candor, he quietly left.

We do not have to respond the way others want us to, and we do not have to be unpleasant just because someone else is acting that way. We can choose how we want to act rather than reacting in knee-jerk fashion. Children, when they say, "He made me do it," are claiming they are not responsible for their own behaviors.

As adults, however, we are completely responsible for everything we do and are capable of making choices about how to act independently of someone else's actions.

Don't let a difficult person drag you down to their level. Choose your own.

Treat Yourself with Respect

No one can make you feel inferior without your consent.
ELEANOR ROOSEVELT

While it is important to treat a difficult person with respect if you want to resolve the difficulties, this does not mean you have to put up with poor treatment yourself. No one has the right to mistreat or be disrespectful to you.

Mistreatment can take many forms. Angry outbursts, put-downs, nasty names, discounting your perceptions and feelings, derisive jokes, changing the subject, blaming, treating your concerns as trivial, giving you orders, forgetting promises, denying that there is a problem, or refusing to discuss problems are all ways that a difficult person can be disrespectful.

You never have to put up with being treated badly. However, as we all know, getting the abuse to stop is not easy. Strengthening self-esteem is always the first step; eventually you will come to realize that you deserve better treatment and be motivated to do something about it.

There is an important distinction between the expression of anger and mistreatment. If someone is angry, he has the right to let you know. What he does not have the right to do is be abusive as his anger is expressed.

Here are some suggestions for dealing with abusive treatment:
- Respond silently to yourself with a reinforcing phrase. Some

of the useful phrases you could repeat to yourself include: "This is not my problem, it's theirs." "I will listen to what is true and ignore the rest." "I am entitled to have my own beliefs and feelings." "I can wait calmly until this is over."

• Imagine that you have an invisible supporter standing behind you, someone you admire who possesses qualities that could help you stand up to the person. Consider enlisting the help of a movie star, a person from history, or a mythical figure—anyone who would not put up with the type of mistreatment you are experiencing.

• Use silent humor. In your mind, picture the other person getting a pie in the face, slipping on a banana peel, or getting a bucket of water over the head.

• Speak firmly and let the person know in advance that certain behaviors are no longer acceptable. You have every right to set limits and indicate what you are unwilling to experience.

• When being mistreated, say to the person: "I can't listen if you talk to me this way." "I do not appreciate being treated this way." "Calm down, I can't pay attention to what you're saying." "I can appreciate that you are angry, but that does not entitle you to treat me this way."

• Say "Stop!" or "Wait!" or "Hold it!" again and again until it has an effect on the other person. It will.

• Identify mistreatment while it is happening. Use phrases like, "That felt like an insult—is that what you intended?" "I was hurt by that remark—if it happens again, this conversation will end." "I feel like I'm not being taken seriously." "Please say that again with a more respectful tone." "It feels to me like you are not listening." "I don't find that funny." "Remarks like that do nothing to improve the situation." "If your nasty comments continue, I will leave."

• Be careful that you are not pulled into a useless argument or shouting match that you cannot win. As we discussed earlier, avoid engaging in the same tactics yourself.

- Walk away or leave if the mistreatment continues after you have warned the person to stop.

Respect goes both ways. Treating the other person with respect will help to resolve the difficulties, but you must insist on being treated with respect yourself if you're not getting it.

Take Care of Yourself

Hey . . . let's be careful out there.

ADVICE GIVEN TO POLICE OFFICERS
AT THE DAILY BRIEFING ON THE
TELEVISION SHOW *Hill Street Blues*

If you want to work things out with a difficult person, an important consideration is safety. While mistreatment can be unpleasant and harmful to one's self-esteem, it is usually not unsafe. However, some difficult people are dangerous, and it may be unwise even to talk with them about the problem. If there is any history or risk of physical violence, you should avoid the encounter, leave immediately, or have another person present.

Some people may not be dangerous in the moment, but talking with them can result in future harm. If someone is vindictive and has power over you, you may want to think twice about talking to her unless you have a source of power yourself. If you do try to discuss the difficulties, she may attempt to make your life more difficult because you have threatened her authority or self-esteem. In such cases, legal action may be your only recourse.

Another category of people to be careful of are those who are ruthless. Some people will do whatever they can get away with and take whatever they can get if they perceive another as weak. Unfortunately, this type of person perceives weakness in anyone who isn't like he is. If someone wants to negotiate in a reasonable fashion and discuss the issues in a balanced way, a ruthless person sees that person as an easy target.

> There are some types of difficult people with whom a face-to-face discussion would probably be unwise.

Responding to Criticism

> *I do not at all resent criticism, even when, for the sake of emphasis, it for a time parts company with reality.*
>
> WINSTON CHURCHILL

I have a friend who has a quality I wish I possessed; she is rarely bothered by criticism. Her philosophy is simple and wise. If the criticism is true, she listens carefully and considers how she might improve herself. If the criticism is false, she ignores it and assumes the critic has problems of his own.

Few of us operate this way. When someone criticizes us, we tend to get upset and defensive. But why?

Criticism hurts because it reveals an unpleasant truth about ourselves that we have been unwilling to acknowledge. In other words, criticism uncovers the flaws that we have tried to hide from ourselves.

If a criticism is entirely false, then we don't react to it. For example, if someone calls us lazy and we know that we're not, then the criticism has no effect. If someone calls us a spendthrift and we know that it's true, then we just sheepishly (or proudly) admit to it. It's the painful in-between qualities, the qualities we have but wish we didn't, that criticism targets and reveals.

In a book about difficult people, Rick Brinkman and Rick Kirschner actually recommend expressing appreciation to someone who provides criticism. If the critic encounters no resistance, he may well stop. One simply needs to say, "Thanks for being honest," or "Thanks for letting me know how you feel." If you want additional clarification, you can always ask for it.

Criticism might hurt, but it also reveals useful information that can help us to learn about ourselves.

Have You Been Contributing to Your Own Difficulties Without Realizing It?

No man is clever enough to know all the evil he does.

LA ROCHEFOUCAULD

A friend named Maureen worked as a fund-raiser. She loved her job and received excellent reviews until her boss left and was replaced by Tricia. Tricia got the job not because she was qualified, but because she had connections. Because Maureen knew a lot more than Tricia did, she became more and more annoyed at Tricia as she was repeatedly told to do things that would have negative repercussions on potential donors.

It didn't take long for Tricia to start dropping some not-too-subtle hints that she wasn't happy with Maureen's job performance. Maureen also found out through some contacts that Tricia had even talked to the human resources department about firing Maureen.

I visited Maureen at work to discuss her situation, convinced Tricia was the sole culprit. But as Maureen happened to walk by Tricia's office, she shot a look of contempt through the door. The hidden source of the problem suddenly became apparent—Maureen's attitude toward Tricia was as much to blame as Tricia's behavior. Maureen's lack of respect for Tricia was obvious to anyone who observed them.

Sometimes, although we may not realize it, when someone continues to act in a difficult way toward us, it is because we are being difficult to that person. Our attitudes and behaviors, whether unconscious or deliberate, can provoke someone to act even more difficult.

Maureen's boss was clearly incompetent. But Maureen soured the relationship by conveying her lack of respect nonverbally. This further provoked Tricia, who was already scared by the daily challenges of a new job that was over her head. Maureen could have overcome her feelings about Tricia and offered to help her new boss "learn the ropes" in a way that strengthened their relationship rather than responding in a way that created more bad feelings.

The key lies in how we respond to a difficult person. While it is natural for us to respond negatively to mistreatment, negativity usually backfires, and the difficulties only escalate. Responding positively can help resolve the difficulties.

You need to ask yourself what, if anything, you might be doing to make things worse.

Approaching the Subject

The real art of conversation is not only to say the right thing in the right place but to leave unsaid the wrong thing at the tempting moment.

DOROTHY NEVILL

If the difficulties have been going on for a while and neither party has talked about them, then it's going to be hard to bring up the subject and harder still to talk about it. Here are some thoughts about initiating the dreaded conversation.

• Let's return to the idea that most of the time the best thing to do is to honestly express one's feelings in the moment. One possible approach would be to say something like, "I've been wanting to talk to you about the problem we're having, and it's been hard for me to bring up the subject. Are you willing to talk with me about it?" The basic idea here is to just describe your feelings and wishes.

• Avoid blame, even if it's clear to you and everyone else that the other person is in the wrong. Starting out with a blaming tone just puts the other person on the defensive. Say something like, "We've been having some difficulties, and I'm hoping you'll be willing to meet with me and talk about them," which doesn't assign blame to the other person.

• Avoid blaming yourself as well, unless you are entirely in the wrong, and you are the difficult person who wants to make amends. By taking initial responsibility for the problem, you put yourself in an inferior, subordinate role, which weakens your ability to convey your feelings and perceptions to the other person effectively. When you take the blame unnecessarily, you are undermining whatever you subsequently say.

• Continue to be honest about what you're feeling. It makes you more human to the other person. If you're nervous, say you're nervous. If you're happy that the person is willing to talk to you, say so. Disclosing one's emotions creates an atmosphere of familiarity and ease.

Initiating a conversation with a difficult person may be awkward, but it's better than the alternative.

Using Truth as a Weapon

A truth that's told with bad intent
Beats all the lies you can invent.

WILLIAM BLAKE

One of the qualities I like to think I possess is the ability to see things that others miss. This has been a liability as much as an asset for me, because when I do see things that others don't, I can be indelicate enough to share my perceptions. Problems arise when the person hearing this isn't receptive. Truth is not always a welcome commodity. I am not always a tactful observer.

Any time we make a statement about another person, we run the risk of imposing an unwelcome form of truth. If I say to you that you're self-centered or you don't keep your promises, what I say may indeed be close to the truth, but it's not necessarily a truth you want to hear. You will probably get defensive and shut out any future comments I might make. You are going to assume that I am accusing you of doing something wrong, and you would be right.

As psychologist Daniel Wile points out, "you" statements tend to be accusatory, regardless of whether they're accurate. They are easy to argue with because they are subjective.

"I" statements, on the other hand, are just expressions of feeling. If I'm your spouse, I might tell you that I felt ignored and shut out of your life when you made the decision to change jobs without discussing it with me, instead of calling you self-centered. Or I might say that I got angry last week when you promised to go to a play with me and then forgot about it instead of accusing you of not keeping promises. In both cases I'm just stating my own truth without accusing you of anything; in both cases what you did is a fact that can't be argued with.

Notice how the earlier "you" statements were restated much more effectively as "I" statements. In actuality, every "you" statement is a general version of a specific "I" statement. When you want to accuse someone of something, there is always a feeling underneath that can be expressed in the following way: "When you do _____, I feel _____."

All this leads to some simple advice about talking to a difficult person. Try not to impose your version of the truth by using "you" statements. Stick to "I" statements that describe your underlying feelings in response to the other person's behavior.

To create a receptive climate for a conversation with a difficult person, avoid accusations and describe your own feelings.

Don't Be So Serious!

Humor brings insight and tolerance.

AGNES REPPLIER

Shortly after college, in my smart-mouthed early twenties, I worked for a start-up telecommunications firm that is now one of the industry giants. Lenny, my frazzled and overworked boss, would periodically bark orders and guzzle coffee sitcom style as he attempted to goad his sales force into meeting the week's quota.

One afternoon he bellowed an order at me. I bowed ever so slowly at the waist, gestured sweepingly with my arm, and said, "Yes, your Highness."

Fortunately, he had a sense of humor. We both laughed at our respective silliness, and he became more reasonable, at least for the rest of the day.

In graduate school, I managed to alienate a professor with whom it was important to stay on good terms. I was not shy about approaching people I'd angered, so I went to his office during office hours. He was surprised at my boldness, and even more surprised when I stated, "I seem to be on your sh*t list—how do I get off?" He paused for a few moments, cocked an eyebrow, smiled, and said, "Well, it's not really a sh*t list, it's more like a fart list." That was the end of our difficulties. My technique was admittedly crude, but it worked.

One well-timed remark with just the right humorous tone can dispel all sorts of unpleasant feelings. Humor has a quality of bringing lightness and release to a serious situation—it is like turning on the light in a dark room.

When we are engaged in a conversation with a difficult person, the tone can be serious and painful and heavy. Humor, as long as it is light-hearted and not sarcastic, can shift the energy and energize the discussion.

There is humor to be found in every situation. Improve your difficult situation by finding it.

When Should You Write?

Why is it that you can sometimes feel the reality of people more keenly through a letter than face-to-face?

ANNE MORROW LINDBERGH

There are people I know who prefer to write a letter to someone with whom they are having difficulties rather than talking. Here are two stories describing what can happen as a result.

Alex, an artist, fell a few weeks behind on his rent for the first time in his life after living in his current apartment for almost five years. He received a nasty letter from his landlady that went beyond a request for money and denigrated his character. Angry about the personal nature of the attack, he knocked on her door and confronted her; she lived in the same building. She responded that she had always written to people when she was upset with them and that was her style. Alex replied that her tactic was an easy way to avoid dealing with the hurt she created in the hearts of those who received her letters.

Craig, a product designer in his forties, opened the mail one day to find a twelve-page, handwritten, single-spaced letter from his brother Brad, who was two years younger. Brad, who had apparently been "working on his issues," outlined in detail all the hurtful things Craig had done to him, going back to the age of four. Craig could barely remember most of them. He felt terrible and didn't know how to respond. He wondered what had inspired his brother to suddenly unload years of pent-up resentment in this fashion.

In the previous chapter we explored the use of writing to heal our emotional hurts and emphasized that writing to communicate requires a different approach than writing to heal. When is it a good idea to write? How should it be done?

Letters are perfect for those who are not articulate and express themselves better on paper. For this type of person, letter writing will help in saying what is hard to verbalize face-to-face. Or for those who want to word their message carefully, a letter offers the luxury of time; one can think, write, and edit, options one doesn't have when talking. Still another reason for writing is to create some distance. It is sometimes hard to communicate with certain people in person because they are demanding or taxing.

Regardless of the reason for writing, what a letter writer lacks, as the stories that begin this section illustrate, is the ability to see how another is affected. When you send a letter, you're not there when it is read and the recipient reacts to it. What this creates is a tempting situation in which you are inclined to say things you would never have the nerve to say to someone's face. What results if you're not careful is an escalation of the problem and more hurt feelings. This is why I do not recommend mailing a letter that one has written to heal one's feelings. It was not written with the other person's reaction in mind and is likely to make the situation worse.

There is another reason that one should be hesitant about sending a letter, and that is its permanence. Words, once spoken, remain only in the memory of the listener. But letters, once written, continue to speak each time they are read and reread.

E-mail as an alternative to letter writing poses its own problems. The ease and immediacy of the medium fosters an even greater risk of acting hastily. In the heat of one's emotions, it is easy to dash off a "flame" and send it before one has had a chance to think about the implications. And E-mail is much too easy to share. A private, intimate, or intense communication can be easily passed along to anyone, anywhere.

So if you want to write, the ideal situation is to hand deliver the letter and have the person read it in your presence. Explain that you feel more comfortable expressing your thoughts and feelings on paper. This serves two purposes. First, it tempers what you write; if you know you're going to be right there when the other person reads what you've written, you're much less likely to get carried away and write something stupid or hurtful. Second, it enables you to immediately see the other person's facial expression and hear his reaction. Then you can talk about the situation and minimize any misunderstandings.

If personal delivery is not possible or practical, perhaps because the person is too difficult to deal with in person, be careful to write your letter or send your E-mail message as if you were going to be there when it is read. Show the communication to several trusted friends before sending it; ask them how they would feel if they received such a message. This will minimize the potential of saying something that makes things worse.

There is another type of situation in which a letter can be helpful. If people are estranged and have been out of touch for a long time, a phone call or personal meeting might be too unexpected and unsettling. A letter can break the silence and begin the process of healing, forgiveness, and reconciliation. The initial letter should be simple, expressing a desire to reconnect and suggesting a face-to-face talk; the origin of the difficulties should not be mentioned.

The simple rule of thumb when writing is to ask yourself how you would feel if you were to receive the letter you are about to send. Your motive when writing for another's eyes should be the same as for a face-to-face talk—to let the other know how you feel as a result of his behavior or to apologize for your own. Letters should never be used for accusations, attacks, denunciations, blame, or vilification.

> Write a carefully worded letter to a difficult person if you feel that you communicate better that way, or if you have not spoken to the person in a long time, or if it is someone too difficult to deal with in person. Don't write to tell the person off.

Allow the Difficulties to Heal over Time

You can't push a wave onto the shore any faster than the ocean brings it in.

SUSAN STRASBERG

In this chapter, we've explored various approaches for talking with or writing to a difficult person. All require us to do something. What we haven't yet considered is doing nothing.

Joanne came to one of my workshops because of strained relations with a sister. She had tried a number of times to talk about their problems without success. Now she was hoping to learn a new strategy that might work.

During an exercise in which we used focusing to gain insight, Joanne's inner wisdom told her, surprisingly, to back off. She realized that she had been too pushy and the best way to heal the difficulties was to just allow time to pass.

The mind and body have natural healing mechanisms that work without conscious effort. When feelings are intense on both sides, allowing them to subside over time may be the wisest course of action. This is a time for silence, not words.

The issue of timing in relationships is one that is often overlooked. There are times when it is appropriate to talk about the difficulties, while at other times talking can only make things worse.

The question, of course, is how does one know when the time is right? This requires us to read the situation carefully. Are we in control of our own emotions, or is there a possibility that we might lose control? Does the other person appear to be receptive or resistant? How urgent are the issues? What else is happening in the other person's life that might divert their energies and attention right now?

Not talking can sometimes be the best course of action.

Avoid Burning Bridges

It ain't over till it's over.

YOGI BERRA

Nasty letters and vengeful acts are ways of nailing the door shut with the difficult person on the outside. When someone has hurt us deeply, we may find ourselves desiring permanent distance.

The problem that arises when we sever relations, leaving an unpleasant aftertaste, is that we only *think* the person is out of our life. He or she might be gone physically but is not gone emotionally. Pain does not go away just because the person does. Out of sight in this case does not necessarily mean out of mind.

There is something else that does not go away just because the person is out of our life, and that is the invisible connection we have to the person in the spiritual realm. When a relationship does not end peacefully, it is said that the two people remain linked in what can be called a trauma bond. The bond is not broken until the difficulties are truly healed.

We discussed at length in chapter 4 the spiritual implications of hurting another or of thinking hurtful thoughts. If we stay angry and resentful, if we hold on to a grudge, we will eventually find ourselves accountable for the negativity we radiate into the world. We may receive it back in the form of health problems or by enduring the pain of another difficult person.

Those who believe in reincarnation make the case that unresolved difficulties carry over into our next life, requiring us to deal with the person once again. The setting is, of course, different, but the issues remain the same. For some believers, this provides an excuse to not deal with the problem. It presents an easy way out, the ultimate in procrastination. But what someone is putting off by not dealing with the difficulties is their own spiritual development and their progress in establishing a relationship with the divine. Now is the time to heal, not in some vague future life. Those who don't believe in reincarnation but do believe in an afterlife would argue that one is accountable for one's ill feelings after death at the time of judgment. Forgiveness forestalls heavenly punishment.

Be careful not to burn bridges behind you in anger. You will eventually have to cross them again in an unexpected and unpleasant way.

A Wounded Heart

The bitterest tears shed over graves are for words left unsaid and deeds left undone.

HARRIET BEECHER STOWE

Sometimes the difficult people in our lives are people we have once loved or may still love. Conflicts arise, hurtful words are spoken, and damaging acts are committed. The love that was once there is denied and replaced with bitterness that can linger for a long time. No type of difficulty between people is more painful than a rift of shattered love.

Outrage, sorrow, anguish, even hate seem justified at the time of the violation. But how long can one continue to feel this way? At what point does one escape these toxic feelings? Who is the rancor really hurting—the person at whom it is directed, or the one who harbors it?

Nothing brings these questions to the forefront more powerfully than death. Once someone has departed this earth, the opportunity to heal, forgive, and reconcile is lost. One has to ask just how important the original issue was to justify the emptiness of being unable to ever heal the rift.

A faculty colleague of mine endured the very worst tragedy one can imagine. One of her twin sons died in a car crash just after his high school graduation. In spite of her immeasurable grief, she took it upon herself as a mission to remind everyone she encountered to hug family members and tell them how much they are loved. She had learned, so very painfully, that loved ones could be gone in an instant with no warning.

One close friend who was estranged from her own teenaged son took the message to heart. The woman reached out, and the two met to begin the process of reconciliation. Several days later, the woman's son drowned attempting to save a friend.

The love that was once there always resides deep within. Work on letting it back into your life, however long that takes and however painful the process will be. Do it before the time comes when it will never again be possible to express it.

Love is forever. Bitterness lasts only as long as we let it.

A Tearful Embrace

Courage is the price that life exacts for granting peace.
The soul that knows it not, knows no release.

AMELIA EARHART

Jacob and Esau, long estranged, reunited in a tearful embrace. There is no emotion like that of forgiveness and reconciliation. The tears that come when one forgives emerge from the innermost chambers of the heart, the place where we are connected to each other and to holiness. To heal a long-standing conflict, to forgive in a purifying release, is a great achievement.

It takes courage to do so. It demands the willingness to experience uncertainty, because one doesn't know how things will turn out. It calls for inner strength to feel and endure one's deepest emotional hurts and fears. It requires wisdom to know what to say, what not to say, and when to say it. It insists on patience to face the other person's intense reactions.

Finally, reconciliation asks us to acknowledge and accept the absurdity of the human condition. It is truly absurd that two people, both created in the image of God, have entirely forgotten this truth about each other. And it is tragic that pain and sadness and turmoil are the result.

To forgive and to reconcile reconnects us to the divine realm that links us all.

Explorations

CLARIFYING YOUR GOALS

Purpose: To identify both obvious and hidden goals prior to a conversation with a difficult person

Before talking to a difficult person, be clear about what you want. This exercise will help.

Step 1   Identify your material goals—what are the tangible, material things or behaviors you want as a result of meeting with the other person? Be specific with respect to such things as dollar amounts, deadlines, or actions. How long will it take? What can you realistically expect now and what will probably have to wait?

Step 2	Identify your relational goals—how do you want the relationship to change? Do you want to be closer or more distant? Do you want more power or are you willing to relinquish some? Do you want decisions to be made jointly or independently? What additional rights do you want or are you willing to give?
Step 3	What are your emotional goals, how do you want to feel about yourself? What feelings are you having now that are unpleasant and make you uncomfortable? What would alleviate them? Do you need an apology and / or an admission of wrongdoing?
Step 4	What are your procedural goals—how do you want things to proceed between the two of you? What process would you like to follow? Who else should be involved? Do you want an informal written agreement? A legal contract? A way to verify that agreements have been kept? No face-to-face contact?
Step 5	Once you've listed all your goals, consider their relative importance. Which are must-haves? Which are desirable but not essential?
Step 6	Now, consider the possibility that you might not get your must-haves. What is your best alternative?

CHAPTER 7

RELATING TO DIFFICULT PEOPLE AS A SPIRITUAL PRACTICE

Relationships and Spiritual Growth

He that loveth not his brother whom he hath seen, how can he love God whom he hath not seen?

I JOHN 4:20

All spiritual growth takes place in the context of a relationship. Quite naturally, most people with a spiritual orientation focus on developing a relationship with the divine, connecting to God through doctrine, prayer, study, or meditation. But spirituality is not solely about embracing a set of "correct" beliefs, worshiping regularly, mastering scripture, or having mystical experiences. Each of these laudable pursuits leads to private truths that enhance one's relationship to the divine but not necessarily to one's fellow human beings.

Humanity surrounds us, while divinity is concealed. Spiritual development, then, must logically also include as a part of one's daily routine the conscious intention to improve one's behavior toward others; each of us is created in God's image.

During my twenty-five years as a spiritual seeker, I have met many people who can recite scripture from memory and who pray or meditate daily. I have talked with people who describe profound mystical experiences. I have heard people insist that their set of beliefs is Truth. I have observed spiritual teachers with many thousands of followers. These are dear and deeply spiritual people. But to my discomfort, I've also observed in some people a rift between inner experience and outer behavior. The latter group have holy intentions, holy knowledge, and even holy experiences but don't necessarily act in holy ways.

It's only fair that if I'm going to pass judgment on others, I must also do so on myself. I am the first to admit that on more than a few occasions my behavior toward others has not been spiritual either.

But these occasions have taught me. Whenever I've come to the realization that I've harmed someone, or whenever I've received uncomfortable feedback from a person I've hurt, I've been motivated to make changes. And my spiritual orientation has shifted as a result. Now I am much less interested in transitory spiritual experiences and abstract scriptural insights. What concerns me far more is becoming a better person. In my clearer moments, I recognize that with each person I encounter, whether loving or difficult, I am interacting with the divine. It's a humbling realization. As spiritual pursuits, meditation and prayer are much easier than attempting to see the divine in a difficult person. However, I've found I grow more from the latter because of the challenge.

We express our spirituality in relationships with others by developing our character and mastering (not suppressing) our emotions. One of the most telling indicators of the authenticity of any spiritual path is the extent to which it develops qualities such as tolerance, self-control, kindness, compassion, gratitude, humility, forgiveness, patience, charitableness, and the desire to serve others.

In this concluding chapter, we explore some of the ways that our daily interactions can help us to cultivate these qualities. We examine how relating to people can be a spiritual practice, and especially how relating to difficult people can provide us with rich opportunities to grow spiritually.

If you are willing to invest time in physical exercise each day in order to feel good, consider adding spiritual exercises toward others each day in order to *do* good.

Self-Knowledge as the Starting Point

A person can live with himself for seventy years and still not know himself.

RABBI YISROEL SALANTER

In the days when I taught meditation, I would give public lectures on the benefits of daily practice for mind, body, and emotions. Every so often, I'd meet someone who declined to learn because he claimed he was entirely happy with the way he was and didn't see any need to change. I never knew whether to be envious or skeptical. To go through life thinking that one is just fine and doesn't need to grow is utterly foreign to my way of thinking.

The fundamental premise of this book is that spiritual development is about growing as a person and that difficult people teach us how to do this. By paying attention to our experiences with difficult people, we learn things about ourselves that wouldn't otherwise come to our awareness.

Acquiring self-knowledge is a prerequisite for any type of self-improvement. How can meaningful change take place if we don't have a good idea of what it is that needs to change? Without a clear sense of our strengths and weaknesses, faults and virtues, we have no foundation for purposeful change. When we acquire self-knowledge, we have a better idea of what to target for improvement.

Self-knowledge also provides the basis for improving our behavior toward others. By knowing ourselves, we acquire more insight into the motivations of others and gain a deeper understanding of their behavior. By becoming aware of our weaknesses, we can be more attentive in our interactions with others and catch ourselves before we do things that might be harmful.

In order for us to acquire self-knowledge, several conditions need to be present. The first is acceptance. We must be able to accept whatever we learn, however uncomfortable or unwelcome the knowledge might be. The quest for self-knowledge can reveal all sorts of things that we would prefer not to know about ourselves. But the alternative, to remain unaware, condemns us to continue along the same course as before, with all its pain and pitfalls.

The second condition is aspiration. We need the desire to learn about ourselves. Without aspiration, we will not be inclined to ask questions, seek information, probe experiences, or solicit feedback from others. Learning about ourselves is similar to any other type of learning; it is not a passive process but requires that we actively pursue knowledge.

The third condition is attentiveness. We must be alert to the meaning behind our experiences. We need to pay attention to thoughts, feelings, behaviors, and reactions to others. By observing our thoughts, we discover what is most important to us and the nature of our desires. By observing our feelings we discover our likes and dislikes, our aversions and attractions. By observing our behaviors toward others and our reactions to others, we uncover our character traits and faults.

The fourth condition is receptivity. We need to admit that we don't have all the answers. We need to recognize that there is always something to be learned; self-discovery is a lifelong process. We need to acknowledge that we can learn from anyone at any time and that other points of view enrich our own.

Self-knowledge is the basis for personal change. Acceptance, aspiration, attentiveness, and receptivity are necessary to acquire it.

Avoiding Judgment

To be aware of a single shortcoming within oneself is more useful than to be aware of a thousand in somebody else.

THE DALAI LAMA

Michelle wears too much makeup. Miguel thinks too highly of himself. Caroline can't be trusted with a secret. Peter is too materialistic. Denise is immature. Tim is irresponsible.

If you were to make a list of the shortcomings of the people in your life, how long would it be, and what would it contain? When you meet someone, is your first inclination to make an assessment based on her skin color, nationality, clothing, overall appearance, mannerisms, or speech? Do you criticize the flaws of others behind their backs or to their faces?

The answer, no doubt, is yes. These are things that we all do. It's almost automatic. Some of us may look for faults more than others do, some of us may be more vocal about what we see, but we all do it.

When you find yourself judging another, a simple trick is to try this suggestion from chapter 4—ask yourself if you do the same thing that you are condemning.

It's not easy to stop judging people. However, it's relatively easy to ask yourself this question. It merely requires a simple linkage between a judging thought and another thought that goes something like, "Oh, there I go, I'm judging again. Hmm, I wonder what this is all about?"

Chances are pretty good that if you're willing to be honest with yourself and spend more time reflecting, you'll learn something valuable. You won't always like what you discover about yourself. But the alternative is to go on judging and avoiding the opportunity to acquire self-knowledge.

The beauty of this approach is that you don't have to struggle to stop being judgmental or kick yourself for being that way. You don't have to try to stifle your impulses. Being judgmental is, in fact, a sort of asset for a person on the path to self-knowledge, because every time you judge someone else, you are potentially opening a window into yourself. The catch is that you have to remember to open it. No one else can.

A spiritual approach toward difficult people does not demand that you stop judging them. Instead, it means honestly asking yourself why you are reacting to them in a judgmental fashion.

Accepting the Situation

We have to love our neighbor because he is there. . . . He is the sample of humanity that is actually given us. Precisely because he may be anybody he is everybody.

G. K. CHESTERTON

I encountered George during one of my stints as a volunteer for a spiritual organization. George, to put it mildly, was strange. A former government employee on a disability, he was terribly gaunt, had an odd demeanor, and was dogmatically rigid about his spiritual practice. Since he didn't have a job, he came in to volunteer every day, alienating everyone with his manner. Things got so bad he was only given tasks in the back office so he wouldn't interact with the public.

At our next scheduled business meeting we put George on

the agenda to decide what to do about him. Some were in favor of asking him to stop coming. In preparation, I meditated and prayed for guidance. What came was surprising and humbling.

The insight that surfaced was that George was there to teach us tolerance, patience, and love. We needed him. And he needed us as well to help him to heal.

I shared my feelings at the meeting; as much as people wanted him gone, they also reluctantly acknowledged the importance of the perspective I brought. So George kept coming every day. We gulped and tried our best to help him and work on ourselves.

From that time on, I always felt that whenever a difficult person came into my life, there was a purpose to his or her appearance. It was not my place to summarily dismiss someone merely because of an oddness that made me uncomfortable. At the same time, there were realistic limits to my tolerance; I had to be careful not to exceed these limits. Ignoring them inevitably led to stress and negative reactions.

The difficult people in our lives are there for reasons we may never understand. But they are there, and unless we are in danger, we need to accept their presence. At the same time, we need to take care of ourselves, and we need to be vigilant so that we don't cause them any harm. It's a delicate balancing act.

There is a story about the mystical teacher Gurdjieff and one of his disciples. The disciple, who lived in the ashram, was strongly disliked by the other disciples for a variety of reasons. When he left, Gurdjieff actually tracked him down and paid him to return, telling the rest of the disciples that the ostracized man was one of their most important teachers.

The next time a difficult person comes into your life, it might be helpful to tell yourself something along the lines of "(Sigh) Here comes another one. God, I ask you to guide me. You have sent this person to me for a reason. Help me to know what it is, and help me to cope successfully."

Assume that difficult people come into your life for a purpose.
Accept their presence, take care of yourself, and pray for guidance.

Seeing the Good in Others

*As the prudent vintager eats only ripe grapes, and gathers
not those which are green, so the eyes of a wise man rest
only upon the virtue in others; whereas the eye of the fool
seeks only to discover in his neighbor vices and defects.*

S A I N T   J O H N   C L I M A C U S

All of us like to be appreciated for our good qualities, and all of us
dislike it when others focus on our negative qualities. Some of us
go to great lengths to avoid having our darker side revealed. It can
be excruciatingly painful when something we are ashamed of is
exposed to the light.

Applying the Golden Rule would suggest that since we don't
wish to have our less laudable qualities emphasized, we shouldn't
emphasize those of others.

But that's exactly what we do when someone is being difficult. We zero in on the behavior that is driving us crazy and immediately describe the person negatively. We cease to see him as a
person with both good and bad traits and view him instead with
one-dimensional vision.

All of us have both good sides and bad sides. All of us. In most,
good dominates; in some, bad dominates. But both coexist. If we
were all good, our soul wouldn't need to come into physical man-
ifestation on earth to learn certain spiritual lessons. And if we
were all bad, our soul would not have earned the right to be here.

We live in a society that searches for flaws in others the way a
doctor scrutinizes an X ray for disease. But focusing on others'
bad points isn't a harmless exercise.

There is now a growing body of scientific evidence that prayer influences healing, which suggests that our thoughts have an influence on other people. When we focus on another person's negative qualities, it is as if our thought energy migrates to that person, and we feed the bad qualities with our negative attention. That only makes the negativity stronger.

By focusing on the good, we strengthen the good. By looking for the good in others, we help them, and at the same time we bring good to ourselves. We also reverse the process of seeing difficult people one-dimensionally and begin to see them as people just like us, with good points and flaws.

The next time you find yourself focusing on a person's negative qualities, remind yourself to look for the good.

Speaking with Sensitivity

The name we give to something shapes our attitude toward it.

KATHERINE PATERSON

With a few carefully or carelessly chosen words, I can either mend my difficulties with another person or damage the relationship further. By describing a person negatively with just a phrase, I can poison others' minds toward him and damage his reputation. Just a brief utterance, spoken rashly, can incite another to violence; a few appropriate words can foster peace.

We talk so readily and words come so effortlessly that it is easy not to realize the devastating or healing effects they can have. There is an Eastern European tale, retold by Joseph Telushkin, about a man who goes through a town, slandering the rabbi. After a change of heart, he approaches the rabbi and asks to be forgiven, offering to do anything to make things right. The rabbi duly instructs him to take a feather pillow, slash it open, and let the feathers fly away in the wind. After following these instructions carefully, the man returns to the rabbi and asks if he has atoned for his wrong. "Not yet," the rabbi tells him, "now you must gather up all the feathers."

The man, aghast, protests to the rabbi that his request is impossible since the feathers have now been blown across the land. The rabbi replies, "Just as it is impossible to retrieve the feathers, so it is equally impossible to undo the damage that your words have created."

Speech has particular relevance in our relationships with difficult people. We often use negative words to describe them, either behind their backs or to their faces. Negative words, however, can foreshadow negative behavior.

Causing deliberate harm to another isn't something most people can just do. Before mistreating or hurting another, one must somehow justify that the other deserves to be harmed. In our legal system, this is accomplished by the pronouncement of guilt in a courtroom. In our personal lives, we accomplish it by labeling a person negatively. Name-calling and nasty labels almost always precede harmful actions.

In one sense, I may have done an injustice to the readers of this book by using the term "difficult person." The phrase implies that there is something wrong with the other person if there is a problem; it gives tacit permission to view that person in a negative way and subsequently treat him or her differently.

Perhaps you may feel this particular choice of words is relatively harmless, but the principle is anything but. History has shown how entire races and nationalities have been horribly persecuted after the dominant group in the society has systematically described them in degrading ways. Before the early church could justify torturing someone who disagreed with accepted teachings, the person had to be officially labeled as a heretic. As another example, one only has to look at the history of African-Americans in the United States and the evolution of the terms used to describe them over the years. Perhaps the most loathsome illustration comes from Nazi Germany, where Jews were described as vermin so that the German populace could get used to the idea of exterminating them.

Much more could be said about this topic. Practically speaking, we are interested in how we can use speech to positively influence our difficult relationships and avert negative behavior resulting from negative speech. Here are some basic suggestions:

• Avoid describing someone in negative terms to others or to the person's face. This creates distance and a justification for mistreatment.

• Avoid reminding someone of his or her negative qualities, weaknesses, failures, or past misdeeds. This evokes feelings of shame in another, which is antithetical to the goal of respect.

• Be reluctant to believe negative characterizations that someone tells you about another; always assume there is a side to the story you haven't heard yet.

• Avoid passing along anything negative that you have heard about another, even if it is true, unless someone else will be harmed by not knowing. Ask yourself what will be accomplished by the telling. Often the only reasons for gossip are to get someone else's undivided attention and gain a feeling of superiority over the subject of the story. Both these effects are transitory. The damage caused by negative speech lingers.

• Avoid the company of those who take pleasure in disparaging others, or at a minimum, express your discomfort at hearing such conversation.

Words are far more powerful than you realize. Choose them carefully.

Mastering Anger

Anger cannot be overcome by anger. If a person shows anger to you, and you respond with anger, the result is disastrous. In contrast, if you control anger and show opposite attitudes—compassion, tolerance and patience—then not only do you yourself remain in peace, but the other's anger will gradually diminish.

THE DALAI LAMA

Each day, in newspapers and on television, we hear about the consequences of unrestrained anger. A single moment of uncontrolled anger, expressed destructively, can devastate a number of lives. It affects the person harmed by the angry explosion, the person who perpetrates the harm, and the family members of both who must live with the aftermath of a rash act over which they had no control.

For this reason, mastering anger is among the most important spiritual lessons one can learn.

It is necessary to say at the outset that mastering anger does not mean that one holds anger in at all costs, and it does not mean that one expresses anger in a cathartic release whenever it is felt. What it does mean is that one expresses anger appropriately, somewhere between the two extremes.

It is also worth mentioning that the benefits of learning how to experience and express anger aren't just confined to relationships; they also have implications for our health. The medical links between hostility and heart disease have been observed for a number of years.

Most of us aren't destructive enough to make the news during our angry moments; at our worst we might get off a few really good zingers at the other person, perhaps saying things we later regret. But that is the point. Anger clouds judgment, and harsh words spoken in anger cannot be taken back. The damage created can be permanent. Spiritually speaking, anger does not justify harming another.

As Joseph Telushkin points out so cogently, "That you feel rage does not entitle you to inflict emotional pain on others any more than feelings of sexual attraction entitle you to rape the source of your attraction."

We've noted that inappropriate anger harms our relationships and our health; it also makes us look bad. No one acquires respect by losing his temper; no one looks good with a red face and bulging veins.

To understand what it means to master anger, there are two important questions we need to answer. Just what is meant by appropriate anger? And how does one handle anger when it arises without letting it get out of control?

Angry behavior is an attention-getting tactic; when someone gets angry, people pay attention. Children and immature adults take advantage of this by throwing temper tantrums to get what they want. Clearly, this is not appropriate anger.

But anger does serve a useful purpose when it sends a message to another person that a particular behavior is unacceptable. Expressing anger to the person who caused you harm is appropriate when it tells her that something she's done is unacceptable and will not be tolerated. And when the message is delivered in an angry voice, it will definitely get the other person's attention, especially if she has ignored earlier comments delivered in a more even tone.

Our other concern is how to deal with anger when it comes up. I have met people who claim that their anger is uncontrollable; a man I once worked closely with would periodically erupt in anger and then claim he had no control over what had happened. I was foolish enough to believe him until an attractive woman began working in the office. The outbursts suddenly stopped. It was obvious that he didn't want to make a bad impression on her; his anger was indeed within his control. Claiming that one's anger is uncontrollable is just an excuse; the person who makes such a claim just doesn't want to control his anger.

There are a number of strategies for handling anger:

• Anger exists in your body; it is a physiological response. Begin to pay attention to the bodily sensations associated with anger; what is going on in your body when you get angry? By developing this awareness over time, you will begin to sense when you are becoming angry before it gets full-blown.

• Whenever possible, express your angry feelings to the person who caused them at the time of the incident, once you have calmed down. Avoiding the conversation, telling others, and engaging in physical activity to vent your anger won't deal with the source of the problem.

• Phrase your conversation in terms of your own feelings. Say, "I am angry about what you did" rather than, "You made me angry." Describe the behavior that triggered your anger.

• If you find yourself getting out of control, leave or end the conversation at once. You can truthfully say to the person, "I am getting very angry. I need to leave right now (and/or end this conversation) before I say or do something I'll regret."

• Psychologist Leonard Felder recommends counting colors if you find yourself getting angry. This is a more sophisticated version of the classic advice of counting to ten. He suggests systematically listing the colors in your environment to a count of twelve. This activates the areas of the brain shut down when one becomes angry.

• Try to get some clarity about why you are angry. Anger is always a secondary emotion that occurs in conjunction with primary feelings such as hurt, fear, loss, abandonment, heartbreak, or shame. What is the real emotion behind your anger?

- Recognize that anger can light a fire for constructive action. Some of the greatest humanitarians in history were motivated by anger to bring about change. Harness your anger in productive ways. Don't use it to get even.
- Anger arises when desires are unfulfilled and others don't act the way we want them to. A spiritual viewpoint would suggest that we don't always get what we want because the Universe has other plans for us. Recognize that frustration and disappointment may have important spiritual purposes for you.
- The more important a situation is, the angrier we get when things don't turn out the way we want. Ask yourself just how important the current situation really is. You will find that often your anger is over trivial matters; the harm your anger may create will be greater than any objective harm resulting from the situation.
- If anger is a big problem for you, keep an anger journal. Every time you get angry, write down the following information: day, time and place, who angered you, what the circumstances were, what you were angry about, what your mood and fatigue levels were at the time, and whether alcohol was involved. Look for patterns. You might, for example, find you only get angry when tired, or when your competence is called into question, or when you have been drinking.
- Consider working on your anger in therapy.

Having mastery over anger is good for your health, your relationships, and your self-esteem. It improves the way others see you.

Responding with Kindness

That best portion of a good man's life,
His little, nameless, unremembered acts
Of kindness and of love.

WILLIAM WORDSWORTH

I have a friend who works in a government office; the environment is unrelenting and unforgiving. When she learned I was writing a book about how to respond to difficult people in a spiritual fashion, she said, "Oh, I hope you're planning to discuss loving-kindness; that's the approach I take at work or I'd never survive."

Responding to difficult people with kindness embodies many of the recommendations we've covered earlier. It is respectful. It is nonjudgmental. It calms another's anger. It is the most healing form of speech. It is the opposite of letting another's behavior dictate yours. It is often unexpected. It expresses compassion for the suffering behind the difficulties. It recognizes the divinity in the other person.

It is also very hard to do.

Practicing kindness toward a difficult person requires that one first practice it toward people who aren't difficult. In other words, kindness cannot be conjured up as simply another technique for dealing with difficult people. It is a habit of the heart, practiced routinely in one's daily life, that is then gradually extended beyond one's comfort zone toward people unlikely to reciprocate.

It is precisely the challenge of being kind to a difficult person who may not appreciate the kindness that brings spiritual merit. As we've stated earlier, the harder the test, the greater the growth.

One day, just after leaving home to go shopping, I couldn't help but notice an older car hobbling through an intersection. It was emitting clouds of brown smoke from under the hood, a sure sign of serious problems. The driver pulled over, and I continued on my way.

After driving a few blocks, I had a sudden impulse to turn around and help. So I did. As I approached the disabled car and pulled behind it, the driver was talking with a woman who happened to be walking by. I asked him if he needed any help, and he barked back, "No!" The woman he was talking to looked at me, shrugged, and said, "I tried, too."

At that point I could have left, but something told me to keep trying. I pulled out my cellular phone and asked if he needed to make a call. He responded in essentially the same way as the first time. So I called the local police to report his disabled car and waited.

After about five minutes had passed, the man apparently calmed down and acknowledged to himself that he needed help. He walked back to my car, asked if he could use my phone, and complimented me on my patience.

Sometimes people are difficult because life is hard. Kindness is what they need from you more than anything else. They need to know that someone cares, even when they engage in difficult behaviors that are likely to promote the opposite reaction. The next time a waiter or store clerk is rude to you, try being kind and see what happens.

Kindness isn't a universal prescription, however. It can backfire with certain types of people. To express kindness toward those who are persistently self-centered, ruthless, or malicious is to be unkind to oneself. These people take advantage of kindness, viewing it as a weakness and as an opportunity for them to take more. In such instances, being kind may just bring about more difficulties. If the difficulties have been going on for a while, and you are being taken advantage of, kindness may not be the best course of action.

Practice kindness each day toward those you meet when they are not being difficult. It will help you to develop the capacity to be kind even when the other person is being unkind to you.

Forgiveness

He that cannot forgive others, breaks the bridge over which he himself must pass if he would ever reach heaven; for every one has need to be forgiven.

GEORGE HERBERT

I have a confession to make. This book is about forgiveness.

When I first conceived of this book, forgiveness was one of the topics I knew I'd need to write about, but in my mind it was not the central theme. But when the book was about half finished, I suddenly had a flash of realization that everything I was writing about was in actuality a facet of forgiveness.

Forgiveness in most people's minds consists of the act of saying "I forgive you" to someone who has hurt them. But to do so when one has not done inner work to heal personal emotions is both superficial and incomplete.

Forgiveness is not something you do for someone else. It is something you do for yourself so that you can move into the future without being burdened by the grievances of the past. Forgiveness allows you to shed your toxic feelings and free yourself of resentments so that the original hurt does not continue to oppress you each day. Granted, you may have been terribly wounded by someone else's actions. But what happened then doesn't have to keep happening in your mind and heart now.

Forgiveness is therefore an inner state, not an outer act. You can forgive someone without ever speaking to them again, although reconciliation is often desirable as well. Forgiveness is a blessed state in which you can let go of the hurt and no longer expect anything from the one who has caused you harm.

Forgiveness is not something that we can strive for. It is something that happens once we have struggled with our own feelings, searched for meaning, and healed. The process may happen overnight or take years.

Even though forgiveness is an inner process that we do for ourselves, it has the capacity to affect the other person as well, in mysterious ways. Here are two illustrative stories.

In the segment on prayer that appeared in chapter 5, I described my graduate-school struggles and how I prayed for guidance in overcoming them. One of the answers I received in my prayers was that I needed to forgive my graduate advisor, the person who was making my life difficult, even though I was filled with rage after enduring seven months of his stonewalling.

Forgiveness was not an easy thing for me to do. I struggled with the forgiveness affirmations described in chapter 5. Three days later, I received a letter from my advisor indicating his willingness to finally cooperate. We had not been in communication for several months.

Buddhist teacher and author Jack Kornfield tells the story of a woman on a retreat who had been struggling much of her life with the aftermath of childhood abuse. Finally she broke through the pain and forgave her abuser in an emotionally intense catharsis. Upon returning home from the retreat, she found a letter from the person who had abused her waiting in her mailbox. They had not been in contact for fifteen years. He had written, asking for her forgiveness, the same day her inner work had culminated.

These stories illustrate the power of forgiving another, but it is important to realize that forgiveness goes both ways. By forgiving others, we also make it easier to be forgiven ourselves for the harmful things we have done. We have all been difficult, too.

Forgiving one who has harmed you liberates you from the emotional prison you have created for yourself. It is a deeply spiritual act.

Gratitude

When sufferings come, utter thanks to God, for suffering draws you near the Holy One.

THE TALMUD

Given the title and topic of this book, it is appropriate to end it on the theme of "thank you."

It is my sincere hope that having read this book, you are now able to see your difficulties with other people in a new and different way. As painful and unwanted as your experiences with difficult people may be, with luck you now realize the possibilities for spiritual growth that they bring.

Thank the Holy One for giving you these opportunities to learn about yourself and overcome your limitations. Be grateful for your suffering, because through it you have become more open and receptive to the divine. Even though you may have been deeply wounded, realize that in your healing you will find holiness.

Finally, with a smile on your face and humor in your heart, say to your adversary with all sincerity, "Thank you for being such a pain!"

Explorations

TWO PRACTICAL SCENARIOS

Purpose: To apply the techniques and perspectives of this book to specific situations

Throughout this book, the exercises at the end of each chapter have taken a particular idea and explored it. This exercise integrates all of them and considers how a variety of approaches might be applied to a specific situation.

Scenario 1: The Nasty Coworker

You are a departmental manager at a software firm. The vice president of your division calls a meeting of all department heads. The manager of another department, with whom you have a testy relationship, attacks you and your department at the meeting, making you look bad in front of your peers and superiors. You leave the meeting infuriated, not knowing what to do.

How would you respond if you were the manager who was attacked? Write down your responses.

Obviously, there is no one response that is correct. Let's explore some options.

Dealing with your anger before you do anything else is paramount. You might consider writing the other manager a letter (remember, this is not a letter that you will be sending), getting some vigorous exercise, or meditating. You need to wait until your anger subsides somewhat before taking the next step.

If you meditated, you may have come up with some insights for the next step. This is a good time to pray for guidance or practice focusing as well.

You'll want to talk face to face with your coworker as soon as possible following the incident, but after your anger has subsided. You might consider sending a polite and neutral memo or E-mail message indicating that you'd like to meet to discuss what happened.

Recognize that you may not receive an apology or acknowledgment of wrongdoing from the other person. Identify your material, relational, emotional, and procedural goals first. Consider whether the person is malicious and assess whether a meeting might actually make things worse.

At the meeting, let the other person know that you were angered by the attack. Use "I" rather than "you" statements. Be specific about what you want, whether it be no further public attacks, an apology, or better communication in the future between the two of you. Emphasize the benefits to your coworker (assuming there are some) of a better working relationship.

Think about why the manager was being difficult. Is his own department doing poorly? Is there something going on in his personal life? Is he someone with low self-confidence who finds everyone threatening? Is there a problem with substance abuse?

Consider the spiritual meanings behind the attack. Is divine justice operating? Have you ever attacked someone else in public? What interpersonal skills do you need to develop? Has this happened before in another context, suggesting a pattern? Does the offending manager have qualities you dislike? Are they qualities that you also possess? Can you restrain your desire to seek revenge when your normal inclination would be to get even?

Scenario 2: The Know-It-All Mother-in-Law

You have been married five years to a wonderful man and have a good marriage. Your mother-in-law, however, always has advice and she never fails to share it with you. Her doctor, hair stylist, and cleaning person are all better than yours. She doesn't like the way you raise your children, your housekeeping style, or your taste in clothing. She is superficially nice, but underneath it is obvious that she thinks her son could have done better. Your husband has told her a number of times that he is not happy with the way she treats you, but it continues nonetheless.

How would you respond if this were your mother-in-law? Write down your responses.

In this scenario, a face-to-face discussion is not likely to be successful since the problem has been going on for a while and she's been asked to stop. Your best approach is to work on yourself. Therapy, prayer, meditation, focusing, blessings, and forgiven affirmations are all suitable approaches. What you want to do is uncover the spiritual meaning in this situation. Why has the Universe sent you this particular lesson? What do you need to learn?

It will also be helpful to understand your mother-in-law's history. Ask your husband or relatives about her past as a way to understand her better. Her need to feel superior stems from an emotional wound, and understanding it will help you to develop compassion. It will be easier for you to endure her behavior if you understand its origins.

In the interim, it may prove helpful to minimize contact. Or you could work on being more kind and loving, not as a way to placate her but as a way to soften her heart. Resist any inclinations to respond in kind or do something that will hurt her.

ACKNOWLEDGMENTS

Writing these acknowledgments has been a humbling experience. My life has been touched by many wonderful people whose help has been essential for bringing this book into existence.

Katherine Boyle was the first person to encourage me to write a book based on the material in my workshops. Thank you, Katie, for getting me started. Ed Vesneske, Jr., and my agent, Ling Lucas, provided valuable editorial advice during this book's early stages; their input is largely responsible for its format. Ling subsequently performed the miracle of getting a book contract in eight days. Her insights into the world of publishing have been invaluable, and she has been a tireless supporter. My editors, Laura Wood and Leslie Meredith, were wonderfully enthusiastic about this book from the very beginning. They patiently endured the many questions and concerns of a first-time author and were encouraging at all stages. I'd also like to thank all the people behind the scenes at Harmony Books that I haven't yet had the pleasure of meeting for doing their jobs so well.

A number of writers, psychotherapists, academics, and experts on religious thought reviewed my completed manuscript and pointed out ways it could be improved. I am very grateful to Jill Adler, Katherine Blake, Judy Kamm, Bill Keenan, Joan Klagsbrun, Vicki LaFarge, Ramsay Raymond, Chaya Sarah Sadeh, Meir Sendor, Mindy Shankman, Janie Slayden, and Janet Zimmern. Meri Fox gave generously of her time to help with a section that unfortunately ended up on the cutting room floor.

The ideas in this book incubated and evolved in my workshops. Interface, Oasis, Wainwright House, and The New York Open Center all provided an opportunity to offer them to the public. I wish to thank Anne Arsenault, Susan Chiat, Adele Heyman, Roger Paine, Anne Parker, and DeLacey Serantos for opening their doors to me.

Ted Anderson served as an insightful teacher and guide for my explorations into the realm of emotions. I want to thank all of those at Muzzey Street over the years for never letting me get away with anything.

I have been blessed with many opportunities to study with deeply spiritual teachers whom I also consider friends. I've learned much from Rabbi Arthur Green, Rabbi Nehemia Polen, Rabbi Meir Sendor, Rabbi Shohama Wiener, and Rabbi David Zeller.

My studies with Jason Shulman have taken my spirituality in new and profound directions. I strongly suspect that future books of mine will reflect his influence. I'd like to thank all of my Society of Souls classmates for their warmth and sharing.

I was fortunate to have a position at a school that truly cares about students, and I was lucky to work with colleagues who love what they do. I thank Joseph Byrnes, Tony Buono, and Aaron Nurick, successive chairs of the Management Department at Bentley College in Waltham, Massachusetts, for their fairness and support. I also want to thank Terry Tierney for all of her help over the years with the myriad details of academic life.

The staff at the Lincoln Public Library in Lincoln, Massachusetts, cheerfully acquired whatever books I requested via interlibrary loan; I must have been their most frequent patron. I am grateful for their assistance.

A number of people helped me to make the sometimes rocky transition from academic to author after I defied conventional wisdom and quit my day job. I want to thank David, Elaine, and Stephen Adler; Marthajoy Aft; Matia Rania Angelou; Ann Asnes; Katherine Blake; Jennifer Butler; Fred Calm; Randall Ferrell;

Joyce and Lev Friedman; Susan Gaskell; Susan Glover; Hananya, Meira, Moshe, and Sharon Goodman; Bill Keenan; Brian and Tricia Kelly; Emily Kossowsky; Beth and David Kupferman; Dan Ladd; Tomar Levine; Aaron, Gail, Jordan, and Ruven Liebhaber; Ed and Sandra Lowenhar; Kate MacPherson; Marty Mirkin; David Osmond; Marilyn Paul; Norman Paul; Chaya Sarah Sadeh; Channah and Nossen Schafer; Louise Treitman; Moshe Waldoks; and Michael Young.

Robert Grieves and Sally Probasco kept me sane and balanced during my years in graduate school, and I am still grateful to them ten years later. My graduate advisor, who will remain nameless, influenced me immeasurably. He helped me to develop my logical thought processes, but more importantly, his behavior inspired me to think deeply about the principles that eventually became the content of this book. Thank you for being such a pain and inspiring this book.

To my brothers Alan and Barry: You have always been quick to point out when I've been a difficult older sibling. I hope I've finally learned how to be a better brother as a result of your feedback. To my nephews and nieces in Jerusalem—Menachem Zvi, Hillel, Tzipi, and Sara—I love you and I can't wait until you are old enough to read this. To my sisters-in-law, Raizi and Bonnie, thank you for being such good partners to my brothers.

My mother passed away as I was working on the final edits for this book, and I am saddened that she did not live to see its publication. She had a wonderful way with people and was always kind and generous to everyone, even when others were difficult to her. I cannot begin to appreciate how she has influenced me.

All of us grow and change, and my father is no exception. Our relationship may have been difficult when I was younger, but in the present day it is loving—at least most of the time. No matter how strange my decisions may have seemed to him, he has always come around to supporting me. Thank you, Dad, for all that you've given me over the years, and for your enthusiastic promotion of this book to half the population of West Rogers Park.

A final expression of gratitude goes to Katherine Blake. Whenever I needed help, advice, support, or companionship, she always was there. She is one of the most talented and competent people I know, and I've learned a great deal from her example. I consider her my most stellar teacher. Thank you, Kathy, for your gifts and your love.

Notes

I have tried whenever possible to identify the sources of the ideas in this book that didn't originate with me; if I have inadvertently neglected to mention any, I apologize for the omission. Complete citations for all the books mentioned can be found in the bibliography that follows.

Chapter 1

What Makes Someone Difficult? In her book *Working with Difficult People*, Muriel Solomon catalogs one hundred difficult types.

Chapter 2

Doing Nothing For a discussion about the influence of mental states on health, see *Mind/Body Medicine: How to Use Your Mind for Better Health,* by Daniel Goleman and Joel Gurin, and *The Health Effects of Attitudes, Emotions, Relationships,* by Brent Q. Hafen et al.

Leaving For highly practical advice about whether to leave a marriage, see *Too Good to Leave, Too Bad to Stay,* by Mira Kirshenbaum.

Change, or Else! In 1959, John R. P. French, Jr., and Bertram Raven published a theory of the bases of social power which is now widely used. This section is based on their theory.

Let's Make a Deal Two excellent books on influence and negotiation tactics are *Getting to Yes,* by Roger Fisher and William Ury, and *Getting Past No: Negotiating with Difficult People,* by William Ury.

Chapter 3

Some Difficult People Are in Emotional Kindergarten I first heard the term *emotional kindergarten* from Robert Grieves of Madison, Wisconsin.

Some Difficult People Have Emotional Wounds See *Reinventing Your Life,* by Jeffrey Young and Janet Klosko, for a detailed discussion of emotional wounds, which they refer to as lifetraps.

Some Difficult People Want Too Much For a thoughtful discussion of greed, see *The Seven Deadly Sins,* by Solomon Schimmel.

Some Difficult People Are Substance Abusers The information in this section is taken from *Synopsis of Psychiatry,* sixth edition, by Harold Kaplan and Benjamin Sadock.

Sick and Tired David M. Luterman has written a wonderful book, *In the Shadows: Living and Coping with a Loved One's Chronic Illness,* that describes what he learned over ten years of coping with his wife's multiple sclerosis.

A Few Are Evil Portions of this section were influenced by M. Scott Peck's fascinating and thoroughly Christian view of evil, *People of the Lie,* and *Facing Evil: Light at the Core of Darkness,* edited by Paul Woodruff and Harry Wilmer.

Giving Difficult People the Benefit of the Doubt For an in-depth exploration of this idea, see *The Other Side of the Story,* by Yehudis Samet. Samet relies heavily on orthodox Jewish teachings, but the insights are universal.

Separating the Person from the Difficulties This section was inspired by Robin Casarjian's book *Forgiveness: A Bold Choice for a Peaceful Heart.*

Chapter 4

The Exquisite Mystery of Relationships Sophie Freud shared this story at a March 1993 conference entitled Coming into Our Own: Mid-Life Choices, Cycles and Second Winds, held at Interface in Cambridge, Massachusetts.

Tests Abraham's attempted sacrifice of Isaac is probably the most analyzed and commented upon of all biblical stories.

Difficult People Teach Us How Our Actions Affect Others Variations on the Golden Rule from different traditions are taken from *World Scripture: A Comparative Anthology of Sacred Texts,* edited by Andrew Wilson.

Is There Divine Justice? The idea that the Creator is a God of both justice and mercy comes from Kabbalah, the Jewish mystical tradition. The idea that divine justice is delayed until we are capable of learning from it is discussed in *The Path of the Upright,* by Moshe Hayyim Luzzatto. For a Tibetan Buddhist discussion of karma, see *The Way to Freedom,* by the Dalai Lama. For a variety of perspectives on karma, see *Karma, Rhythmic Return to Harmony,* edited by V. Hansen, R. Stewart, and S. Nicholson.

Difficult People Teach Us to Be Cautious For a comprehensive and sobering discussion of cults, see *Cults in Our Midst,* by Margaret Thaler Singer with Janja Lalich.

Difficult People Give Us an Opportunity to Teach Others This concept comes from the book *Why Me God?* by Lisa Aiken.

Difficult People Let Us Know We're Loved Beverly Flanigan's wonderful book *Forgiving the Unforgivable* brought this important idea to my awareness.

Difficult People Serve as Mirrors The idea that God gives us our flaws as well as our talents first came to my attention at a profound workshop on the nature of suffering entitled Kabbalah and Ecstasy, developed and taught by Jason Shulman. For information call 973/538–7689.

Difficult People Help Us to Rectify the Distant Past Psychiatrist Brian Weiss has written several accessible books on reincarnation if you want to explore the concept further. See *Many Lives, Many Masters, Through Time into Healing,* and *Only Love Is Real.*

Chapter 5

Experiencing Intense Emotions *The Anger Workbook,* by Lorraine Bilodeau, is a good place to start when dealing with intense feelings. Psychologist Jeffrey Kottler devotes an entire chapter to the value of emotional pain in his book *Beyond Blame.*

Using Physical Activity to Release See *The Language of Tears,* by Jeffrey Kottler, for a detailed discussion of crying.

Using the Body to Heal I am grateful to Peter S. Churchill for his help with the concepts in the section on bodywork. Peter is nationally certified in therapeutic massage and bodywork and is one of the instructors in Harvard

Medical School's course on alternative medicine. For additional information about bodywork, I recommend *Bodywork: What Type of Massage to Get—and How to Make the Most of It,* by Thomas Claire. For information about breathwork, see *Conscious Breathing,* by Gay Hendricks. Andrew Weil's book *Spontaneous Healing* discusses the role of breath in health and presents several breathing exercises. For information about focusing, see Eugene Gendlin's book, *Focusing.* Focusing classes are offered throughout the world; for information on classes in your area contact the Focusing Institute (United States telephone: 914/362–5222; E-mail: info@focusing.org). For a comprehensive discussion of psychological healing and the body, see *At the Speed of Life,* by Gay and Kathlyn Hendricks.

Individual Therapy The goose story appears in *Depth-Oriented Brief Therapy,* by Bruce Ecker and Laurel Hulley, pages 5 and 10. For a discussion of unconventional therapies, see *Crazy Therapies,* by Margaret Thaler Singer.

Looking to Dreams for Guidance I am grateful to Ramsay Raymond for her help with the concepts in this section. Ramsay is director of The Dreamwheel, a center for the cultivation of dreamwork located in Concord, Massachusetts. For additional information about dreams, two books by the Reverend Jeremy Taylor, past president of the Association for the Study of Dreams, are especially well written: *Dream Work* and *Where People Fly and Water Runs Uphill—Using Dreams to Tap the Wisdom of the Unconscious.*

Meditation Meditation is best learned from a teacher rather than a book. Nevertheless, there are a number of books on the subject. Two books to start with are *The Meditative Mind,* by Daniel Goleman, and *Wherever You Go, There You Are,* by Jon Kabat-Zinn. For information on Christian centering meditation, see *Open Mind, Open Heart,* by Thomas Keating. The past few years have seen a resurgence of interest in Jewish meditation. Recent books on the subject include *The History and Varieties of Jewish Meditation,* by Mark Verman; *The Practice of Kabbalah,* by Steven A. Fisdel; and *The Way of Flame,* by Avram Davis. The classic book on the subject is *Jewish Meditation,* by Aryeh Kaplan.

Praying for Guidance *Your Word Is Fire,* by Arthur Green and Barry Holtz, is a rich book about Jewish prayer that has influenced my practice. I thank Meir Sendor for his help with this section.

Blessings I am grateful to Janet Zimmern of Cambridge, Massachusetts, for her help with this section. The material is drawn from a workshop she developed entitled May You Be a Blessing.

Inner Work and Outer Play Some of these suggestions are adapted from Beverly Flanigan's book *Forgiving the Unforgivable*. *How Can I Help?*, by Ram Dass and Paul Gorman, is a warm and caring book about helping others.

A Diary of Dealings with a Difficult Person If you are interested in keeping a journal, I suggest reading Christina Baldwin's classic book *One to One: Self-Understanding Through Journal Writing*.

Three Healing Letters After recommending for years during my workshops that people write a letter to a difficult person without mailing it, I discovered the same approach in a delightfully unexpected place. Rabbi Kalonymus Kalman Shapira, a saintly Hasidic master who continued to teach in the Warsaw ghetto during the worst period of Nazi oppression, recommended in his 1932 book, *A Student's Obligation,* that a student having difficulty with a fellow student should "write him a letter (but don't send it!). . . . Heap scorn on him, as much as your venomous heart desires; for several days read the letter out loud, while imagining that you are facing him and reviling him with those words of abuse. After some days of this, no doubt your anger will leave your heart, and . . . you will hasten to reconcile with him." This translated passage is taken from page 3 of *The Holy Fire,* Nehemia Polen's deeply moving book about Rabbi Shapira. The idea for the second of the three letters comes from both *Forgiveness,* by Sidney and Suzanne Simon, and *Forgiving the Unforgivable,* by Beverly Flanigan.

Asking for Blessings from Others; Blessing a Difficult Person Again, I wish to thank Janet Zimmern for her help with these exercises.

Chapter 6

I thank Janet Zimmern for suggesting this chapter's title.

A Biblical Tale of Reconciliation All references to Genesis are from Everett Fox's remarkable translation of the Five Books of Moses, which attempts to preserve the rhythms, cadences, wordplay, and style of the original Hebrew. The dual translation of wrestle and embrace for the Hebrew word *vayeyaveyk* was raised by Avivah Gottlieb Zornberg in God Wrestling, Episode 9 of Bill Moyers's PBS television series "Genesis."

The Need to Talk I found chapter 7 of *Interpersonal Conflict,* by Joyce L. Hocker and William W. Wilmot, helpful in thinking about this section.

What Do You Want from the Other Person? This discussion draws from chapter 3 of *Interpersonal Conflict,* by Joyce Hocker and William Wilmot. I have taken the liberty of changing some of their terms.

And Now for Something Completely Different I credit Jeffrey Kottler's book, *Beyond Blame,* for inspiring this section, although his approach is probably more reserved than mine.

Make Sense of the Other Person's Point of View This discussion draws from *The 7 Habits of Highly Effective People,* by Stephen Covey; *People Skills,* by Robert Bolton; and *Organizational Behavior: An Experiential Approach,* fifth edition, by David Kolb et al.

Put the Difficulties in Perspective The story about the parking-lot attendant is taken from a chapter by Gregg Krech entitled *Kyoryoku: The Application of Morita and Naikan Principles to the Work Setting,* which can be found in *Flowing Bridges, Quiet Waters,* by David K. Reynolds. Morita and Naikan are Japanese psychotherapies; this discussion draws upon Naikan, which advocates meditative reflection to help recognize the specific, concrete, ongoing benefits we receive from those around us. Often, we are not appreciative or attentive to what we receive.

Don't Let the Other Person's Behavior Dictate Yours The newsstand story is one I recall reading many years ago, but I can't remember where. I would appreciate learning its origin if any reader knows.

Treat Yourself with Respect See *The Verbally Abusive Relationship,* by Patricia Evans, for detailed advice about how to respond to mistreatment.

Responding to Criticism Rick Brinkman and Rick Kirschner are the authors of *Dealing with People You Can't Stand.* Their discussion of criticism can be found on pages 66–68.

Using Truth as a Weapon Daniel B. Wile is the author of *After the Honeymoon: How Conflict Can Improve Your Relationship.* His insightful discussion of "you" statements and "I" statements can be found on pages 70–73.

When Should You Write? I want to thank Leonard Stein, a professor of psychiatry at the University of Wisconsin-Madison, who first suggested to me the idea of hand delivering a letter and waiting while the recipient reads it.

Avoid Burning Bridges The term trauma bond comes from Henriette Anne Klauser's book *Put Your Heart on Paper.*

Chapter 7

Self-Knowledge as the Starting Point This section draws from *Gateway to Self-Knowledge*, by Zelig Pliskin.

Speaking with Sensitivity The pillow story appears on page 3 of *Words That Hurt, Words That Heal*, by Joseph Telushkin. It is a book I recommend highly.

Mastering Anger The quote is taken from page 72 of *Words That Hurt, Words That Heal*, by Joseph Telushkin. The counting colors technique is described on pages 36–40 of *Does Someone at Work Treat You Badly?*, by Leonard Felder. The idea for an anger journal comes from page 211 of *Gateway to Happiness*, by Zelig Pliskin. This section also draws from *Overcoming Hurts and Anger*, by Dwight Carlson; *The Anger Workbook*, by Lorraine Bilodeau; and *Interpersonal Conflict*, by Joyce Hocker and William Wilmot.

Responding with Kindness *Lovingkindness*, by Sharon Salzberg, treats this topic from a Buddhist perspective. Even so, much of the information is universal. The exercises are especially rich.

Forgiveness There are over seventy books about forgiveness. I recommend the following: *Forgiveness: A Bold Choice for a Peaceful Heart*, by Robin Cassarjian; *Forgiving the Unforgivable*, by Beverly Flanigan; *To Forgive Is Human*, by Michael McCullough, Steven Sandage, and Everett Worthington, Jr.; *Forgiveness: How to Make Peace with Your Past and Get on With Your Life*, by Sidney and Suzanne Simon. The Jack Kornfield story comes from page 281 of his book, *A Path with Heart*. I thank Jean Callahan for bringing it to my attention.

Bibliography

Adahan, Miriam. *It's All a Gift*. Jerusalem: Feldheim Publishers, 1992.

―――. *Living with Difficult People (Including Yourself)*. Jerusalem: Feldheim Publishers, 1991.

Aho, James. *This Thing of Darkness: A Sociology of the Enemy*. Seattle: University of Washington Press, 1994.

Aiken, Lisa. *Why Me God?: A Jewish Guide for Coping with Suffering*. Northvale, N. J.: Jason Aronson, 1996.

Baldwin, Christina. *One to One: Self-Understanding Through Journal Writing*. New York: M. Evans, 1991.

Barreca, Regina. *Sweet Revenge*. New York: Harmony Books, 1995.

Bilodeau, Lorraine. *The Anger Workbook*. Center City, MN: Hazelden, 1992.

Bodine, Echo L. *Passion to Heal: The Ultimate Guide to Your Healing Journey*. Mill Valley, CA: Nataraj Publishing, 1993.

Bolton, Robert. *People Skills*. New York: Simon & Schuster, 1979.

Borysenko, Joan. *Fire in the Soul*. New York: Warner Books, 1993.

Brigham, Deirdre Davis, with Adelaide Davis and Derry Cameron-Sampey. *Imagery for Getting Well*. New York: W. W. Norton, 1994.

Brinkman, Rick, and Rick Kirschner. *Dealing with People You Can't Stand: How to Bring out the Best in People at Their Worst*. New York: McGraw-Hill, 1994.

Bstan-'dzin-ryga-mtsho, Dalai Lama XIV. *Awakening the Mind, Lightening the Heart*. New York: HarperSanFrancisco, 1996.

―――. *Freedom in Exile: The Autobiography of the Dalai Lama*. New York: HarperCollins, 1990.

―――. *The Way to Freedom*. New York: HarperSanFrancisco, 1994.

―――. *The World of Tibetan Buddhism: An Overview of Its Philosophy and Practice*. Boston: Wisdom Publications, 1995.

Buxbaum, Yitzhak. *Jewish Spiritual Practices*. Northvale, NJ: Jason Aronson, 1990.

Carlson, Dwight. *Overcoming Hurts and Anger*. Eugene, OR: Harvest House, 1981.

Carlson, Richard, and Benjamin Shield (eds.). *Healers on Healing*. Los Angeles: Jeremy P. Tarcher, 1989.

Casarjian, Robin. *Forgiveness: A Bold Choice for a Peaceful Heart*. New York: Bantam, 1992.

Claire, Thomas. *Bodywork: What Type of Massage to Get—and How to Make the Most of It*. New York: William Morrow, 1995.

Covey, Stephen R. *The 7 Habits of Highly Effective People*. New York: Simon & Schuster, 1989.

Davis, Avram. *The Way of Flame*. New York: HarperCollins, 1996.

Ecker, Bruce, and Laurel Hulley. *Depth-Oriented Brief Therapy*. San Francisco: Jossey-Bass, 1996.

Evans, Patricia. *The Verbally Abusive Relationship*, second edition. Holbrook, MA: Adams Media Corporation, 1996.

Faraday, Ann. *The Dream Game*. New York: Harper & Row, 1974.

————. *Dream Power*. New York: Coward, McCann & Geoghegan, 1972.

Felder, Leonard. *Does Someone at Work Treat You Badly?* New York: Berkley, 1993.

Fisdel, Steven A. *The Practice of Kabbalah*. Northvale, NJ: Jason Aronson, 1996.

Fisher, Roger, and William Ury, with Bruce Patton. *Getting to Yes: Negotiating Agreement Without Giving In,* second edition. New York: Penguin Books, 1991.

Flanigan, Beverly. *Forgiving the Unforgivable*. New York: Macmillan, 1992.

Fox, Everett. *The Five Books of Moses: Genesis, Exodus, Leviticus, Numbers, Deuteronomy: A New Translation with Introductions, Commentary, and Notes*. New York: Schocken Books, 1995.

Garfield, Patricia. *Creative Dreaming*. New York: Ballantine, 1974.

Gendlin, Eugene T. *Focusing*. New York: Bantam, 1981.

Goleman, Daniel. *Emotional Intelligence*. New York: Bantam, 1995.

————. *The Meditative Mind: The Varieties of Meditative Experience*. Los Angeles: Jeremy P. Tarcher, 1990.

————, and Joel Gurin. *Mind/Body Medicine: How to Use Your Mind for Better Health*. Yonkers, NY: Consumers Union, 1993.

Green, Arthur. *Seek My Face, Speak My Name: A Contemporary Jewish Theology*. Northvale, NJ: Jason Aronson, 1992.

————, and Barry Holtz. *Your Word Is Fire: The Hasidic Masters on Contemplative Prayer.* Woodstock, VT: Jewish Lights Publishing, 1993.

Hafen, Brent Q., Kathryn J. Frandsen, Keith J. Farren, and Keith R. Hooker. *The Health Effects of Attitudes, Emotions, Relationships.* Provo, UT: EMS Associates, 1992.

Hansen, V., R. Stewart, and S. Nicholson (eds.). *Karma, Rhythmic Return to Harmony,* third edition. Wheaton, IL: Quest Books, 1990.

Hendricks, Gay. *Conscious Breathing: Breathwork for Health, Stress Release, and Personal Mastery.* New York: Bantam, 1995.

————, and Kathlyn Hendricks. *At the Speed of Life.* New York: Bantam, 1993.

Hocker, Joyce L., and William W. Wilmot. *Interpersonal Conflict,* fourth edition. Madison, WI: Brown and Benchmark, 1995.

Kabat-Zinn, Jon. *Wherever You Go, There You Are: Mindfulness Meditation in Everyday Life.* New York: Hyperion, 1994.

Kaplan, Aryeh. *Jewish Meditation.* New York: Schocken Books, 1985.

Kaplan, Harold I., and Sadock, Benjamin J. *Synopsis of Psychiatry,* sixth edition. Baltimore: Williams and Wilkins, 1991.

Keating, Thomas. *Open Mind, Open Heart: The Contemplative Dimension of the Gospel.* New York: Amity House, 1986.

Keen, Sam. *Faces of the Enemy: Reflections of the Hostile Imagination.* San Francisco: Harper & Row, 1986.

Kirshenbaum, Mira. *Too Good to Leave, Too Bad to Stay.* New York: Dutton, 1996.

Klauser, Henriette Anne. *Put Your Heart on Paper.* New York: Bantam, 1995.

Kolb, David A., Irwin M. Rubin, and Joyce Osland. *Organizational Behavior: An Experiential Approach,* fifth edition. Englewood Cliffs, NJ: Prentice Hall, 1991.

Kornfield, Jack. *A Path with Heart.* New York: Bantam, 1993.

Kottler, Jeffrey. *Beyond Blame.* San Francisco: Jossey-Bass, 1994.

————. *The Language of Tears.* San Francisco: Jossey-Bass, 1996.

Lang, Denise. *How to Stop Your Relatives from Driving You Crazy.* New York: Fireside, 1990.

Luterman, David M. *In the Shadows: Living and Coping with a Loved One's Chronic Illness.* Bedford, MA: Jade Press, 1995.

Luzzatto, Moshe Hayyim. *The Path of the Upright,* translated by Mordecai M. Kaplan. Philadelphia: Jewish Publication Society of America, 1936.

McCullough, Michael E., Steven J. Sandage, and Everett L. Worthington, Jr. *To Forgive Is Human.* Downers Grove, IL: InterVarsity Press, 1997.

Miller, D. Patrick. *A Little Book of Forgiveness.* New York: Viking, 1994.

Moyers, Bill D. *Genesis: A Living Conversation.* New York: Doubleday, 1996.

Norwood, Robin. *Why Me, Why This, Why Now: A Guide to Answering Life's Toughest Questions.* New York: Carol Southern Books, 1994.

Peck, M. Scott. *People of the Lie.* New York: Simon & Schuster, 1983.

Pliskin, Zelig. *Gateway to Happiness.* Brooklyn: Z. Pliskin, 1983.

————. *Gateway to Self-Knowledge.* Brooklyn: Benei Yakov Publications, 1986.

Polen, Nehemia. *The Holy Fire.* Northvale, NJ: Jason Aronson, 1994.

Ram Dass and Paul Gorman. *How Can I Help?* New York: Alfred A. Knopf, 1985.

Reynolds, David K. *Flowing Bridges, Quiet Waters.* Albany, NY: State University of New York, 1989.

Ruskan, John. *Emotional Clearing.* New York: R. Wyler, 1993.

Salzberg, Sharon. *Lovingkindness.* Boston: Shambhala Publications, 1995.

Samet, Yehudis. *The Other Side of the Story.* Brooklyn: Mesorah Publications, 1996.

Schimmel, Solomon. *The Seven Deadly Sins: Jewish, Christian and Classical Reflections on Human Nature.* New York: The Free Press, 1992.

Simon, Sidney B., and Suzanne Simon. *Forgiveness: How to Make Peace with Your Past and Get on with Your Life.* New York: Warner Books, 1990.

Singer, Margaret Thaler. *Crazy Therapies: What Are They? Do They Work?* San Francisco: Jossey-Bass Publishers, 1996.

————. *Cults in Our Midst.* San Francisco: Jossey-Bass, 1995.

Solomon, Muriel. *Working with Difficult People.* Englewood Cliffs, NJ: Prentice-Hall, 1990.

Taylor, Jeremy. *Dream Work.* Ramsey, NY: Paulist Press, 1983.

————. *Where People Fly and Water Runs Uphill—Using Dreams to Tap the Wisdom of the Unconscious.* New York: Warner Books, 1992.

Telushkin, Joseph. *Words That Hurt, Words That Heal.* New York: William Morrow, 1996.

Ury, William. *Getting Past No: Negotiating with Difficult People.* New York: Bantam, 1991.

Van de Castle, Robert L. *Our Dreaming Mind.* New York: Ballantine, 1994.

Verman, Mark. *The History and Varieties of Jewish Meditation.* Northvale, NJ: Jason Aronson, 1996.

Viscott, David. *The Language of Feelings.* New York: Pocket Books, 1976.

Weil, Andrew. *Spontaneous Healing.* New York: Alfred A. Knopf, 1995.

Weiss, Brian. *Many Lives, Many Masters.* New York: Simon & Schuster, 1988.

————. *Only Love Is Real.* New York: Warner Books, 1996.

————. *Through Time into Healing.* New York: Simon & Schuster, 1992.

Welwood, John. *Love and Awakening: Discovering the Sacred Path of Intimate Relationship.* New York: HarperCollins, 1996.

Wile, Daniel B. *After the Honeymoon: How Conflict Can Improve Your Relationship.* New York: John Wiley, 1988.

Wilson, Andrew (ed.). *World Scripture: A Comparative Anthology of Sacred Texts.* New York: Paragon House, 1991.

Woodruff, Paul, and Wilmer, Harry A. *Facing Evil: Light at the Core of Darkness.* LaSalle, IL: Open Court, 1988.

Young, Jeffrey E., and Janet S. Klosko. *Reinventing Your Life.* New York: Dutton, 1993.

Zweig, Connie, and Jeremiah Abrams (eds.). *Meeting the Shadow.* New York: Jeremy P. Tarcher, 1991.

A NOTE FROM THE AUTHOR

If any of the viewpoints, practices, and techniques recommended in this book have helped you with a difficult person, I would like to hear your story. I am especially interested in stories of healing and reconciliation that have a spiritual element.

Please provide as much detail as possible about the people in the story, what transpired, and how healing and reconciliation occurred. I regret that it will not be possible to acknowledge receipt of your story.

Be sure to include your name, address, and telephone. You will be contacted for permission if your story is used in a future book.

Send your stories to:

Mark I. Rosen
P. O. Box 194
Lincoln, MA 01773

Thank you!

Index

Index

Index